The OTHER SIDE of the Story

DONALD E. BATTLE

Lithonia, GA

© 2018 Donald E. Battle

All rights reserved.

No part of this publication may be reproduced, stored in a retrieval system or transmitted in any form or by any means, electronic, mechanical, photocopying, recording or otherwise, without the expressed written permission of the publisher.

Scripture references are taken from various versions and translations of the Holy Bible. Pronouns for referring to the Father, Son and Holy Spirit are capitalized intentionally and the words satan and devil are never capitalized.

Publisher:
MEWE, LLC
www.mewellc.com

First Edition
ISBN: 9780998828176

Library of Congress Control Number: 2017913499

Printed in the United States of America.

Dedication

This book is dedicated to my dear wife, Gwen, for walking with me every step of the journey and for believing God in every way.

To my children, grandchildren and my DFMI Church family.

Table of Contents

Foreword ix

Introduction xi

Chapter 1 – You Have Authority 1

Chapter 2 – It's in the House 15

Chapter 3 – Have You Been Sifted Yet? 39

Chapter 4 – What's in Your Nothing? 67

Chapter 5 – You Are a Diamond 83

About the Author 101

Foreword

Bishop Donald Battle's book, *The Other Side of the Story*, comes from the crucible of life on the front lines of conflict in gospel ministry. When he challenges you to look at your circumstances from a different perspective, he speaks from his own experience.

For over twenty years, I have watched him walk victoriously through seasons of difficulty time after time. I have witnessed him extend his faith to its fullest, believe God for the impossible and then see the manifestation of God's promises.

Bishop Battle has been a true companion in labor with me, traveling, preaching and helping me in large and small ways for two decades. He has repeatedly sacrificed time at his own ministry and with his family to provide invaluable assistance just when I needed it most.

His wife Gwen is a steadfast and stalwart support to him and an example of a woman who looks well to the ways of her household, as Proverbs 31:27 says. Their entire family is a testimony to the miracle working power of God and hold a special place in my heart.

In this book, not only does Bishop Battle show you what is on the other side of life—he helps you get there yourself by means of the timeless truths of the Word of God. If you are tired of listening to the same old songs of defeat and denial, I encourage you to hear what is playing on the other side — the victory side. Instead of defeat, discouragement and despair, *The Other Side of the Story* will help you attune your spirit to hear a new sound coming from heaven—one that will lead you to fulfillment and success.

Dr. Rod Parsley
Senior Pastor and Founder
World Harvest Church
Columbus, Ohio

Introduction

The story of how I came into ministry began nearly 30 years ago when God revealed the calling He placed on my life. I was married to a beautiful woman who owned a successful business, and we had three lovely daughters living in a spacious home in the suburbs of South Atlanta.

I was content in my career working as one of Atlanta's premier sex crime detectives and took great pleasure in bringing perpetrators to justice. There was always a strong desire within me to save lives and to bring justice and restitution to those who were treated unfairly.

Even though my wife and I had built a very decent life for our family, something within me was still missing. I began to realize that although I had a noble career, it wasn't the fullness of the greater plan God had in store for me. However, when I accepted the call to pastor, I didn't realize the level of sacrifice my family would endure as I moved further into purpose.

In a matter of years, I went from having more than enough in a profitable business and owning my own home to being bankrupt and renting a house behind the church my family attended. All the material possessions I heavily relied upon seemed to be stripped away. It was during this season that I began to recognize that God alone had to be my source of supply and that no matter what, He would take care of me.

I thank God for every personal experience, good and bad, that I have had since responding to His call to ministry. The lessons I have learned along the way have solidified my purpose and strengthened my faith in God's divine blueprint. Little did I know that God was using every lesson to prepare me and my family for something greater.

Life is full of choices, and there are two sides to every situation. We can choose to live on one side or the other. Have you considered discovering the other side of your story? Have you ever thought about what your life could become, and how God could take something seemingly broken and make it beautiful?

You will agree with me that there are always two sides to every story. However, it is true that most of the time you only hear one side. Sometimes, a family member, a friend or even a complete stranger will share a situation about something that happened to them, but they will only tell what they want you to hear.

Over the years, in my role as a pastor, I have had to be intentional when dealing with couples. I do my best to not offer counsel to couples on an individual basis, but to meet with them together. Why? Because I have seen on these occasions how the blame game can be magnified, "it was his or her fault." Yes, after 28 years in ministry, I have truly learned a lot about people and, in the process, I have also learned to hear what is being said as well as to 'hear' what is *not* being told. As a leader, it is important not to rush or be too quick to make judgement calls, especially if I have not heard both sides of the matter. It has also been well said that there are two sides to every story and then there is the *truth* of the matter!

As we live out each day, we know there is right and wrong, there is black and white, love and hate, faith and fear, hope as well as despair. Just like there are two sides to every coin and when tossed it will land on one side only. In life, we are all living a story of our own, one which we often view from a one-sided perspective. This can sometimes result in people living life where they are at, and not where they could or need to be.

There are some things that happen in life that we cannot alter, nor can we change. Things have happened that we can do absolutely nothing about. Situations we cannot go back and fix or even correct. So, all we can do is to accept it for what it is and move on to "better" days!

Long before the digital age of music, we had to purchase a 45-vinyl record from the music store to own a copy of the popular songs of the day. The A-side always featured the 'hit' song that you would see on television or hear on the radio. The B-side would usually remain obscure because those songs got little or no airplay. At first you really didn't care much about what was on the B-side because the 'hit' song is what you really wanted to hear.

Yes, there are some songs I would put on repeat and listen to over and over again. Why? Either because it made me feel good or I just liked what I heard.

I have also found that there is something about repetition that connects us to what we hear and sometimes while listening to the same song repeatedly, after a while I was intrigued to see what was on the other side of the track. Often, I would discover an element of surprise on the B-side that was just as good or sometimes far better than the hit song.

Such is life. If you are not living your best life, there comes a time when you need to make a decision to stop playing the same tune over and over again and flip the script.

Yes, you may have gone through some major difficulties in life that has left you feeling like your story could not possibly get any worse. It may even seem like some things are on repeat. But that does not mean you should throw in the towel and give up. Like your music single, you need to skip to the next track. There's another side to your life; one of renewal and restoration that God can turn around and revive in ways you never dreamed possible.

Today, you may find yourself overwhelmed with debt. You may be going through a divorce or trying to mend a broken relationship. You may be dealing with sickness or feelings of guilt, shame and hopelessness from bad decisions you made in the past. Quite frankly, whatever it is, it happened, and it's time to move on. You cannot let past mistakes define who you are right now. Take it from me, you are not your mistakes. Although you may not be able to see the 'other side' of your current portrait or even have an idea how to get where you need to be, you can rest assured there's a light at the end of every tunnel. I have had many personal experiences that seemed hopeless, but I have also seen God turn those impossible situations around, even transforming an ugly duckling into a beautiful swan!

I can assure you, the problems you encounter today do not have to be permanent. Every hardship in your life is designed to facilitate the discovery of your purpose in the earth. It is the 'other side' of your circumstances that propels you into your God-ordained destiny. But you cannot attain these heights with a narrow or a closed mindset. As the saying goes, "Life is what you make it."

Therefore, we learn and grow as we go. If you want to succeed, you must open your mind to a new way of thinking. Change your outlook on life. Put your faith in God. Release your fears to Him and prepare yourself to step up and step out!

God wants you to give yourself the gift of possibilities by seeing yourself on the 'other side' of your situation. You are not a victim. God wants you to step into your place of victory, and He will walk with you all the way. *"Behold, I am the Lord, the God of all flesh: is there anything too hard for me?"*

(Jeremiah 32:27). *"I will never leave you nor forsake you"* (Hebrews 13:5).

There is no situation that is beyond God's ability to rescue you. Nothing is too hard for Him to accomplish in your life. God is a barrier breaker.

You are a precious gem in the making. You are unique, full of character, and created in God's image. He is at work in and through you, nudging you to untangle yourself from the constraints that have been holding you back. Let something new and better enter your life so you can breathe, soar like an eagle, live and shine like the star God created you to be!

My prayer and desire for you is to see beyond your present position and look forward to your future triumphs. I do believe that you can draw strength from my own life experiences. You will find answers to your questions and see beyond the pain. If you do, then I can honestly say that each lesson I have learned in my past was worth it because they now enable me to speak wisdom into your future!

The *Other Side of the Story* was written to help transform your thoughts and motivate you to reach for everything God has destined for you. You will begin to move toward better things as you understand God's purpose for your life.

> *Then they cry unto the Lord in their trouble, and he saveth them out of their distresses. He sent his*

word, and healed them, and delivered them from their destructions (Psalm 107:19-21).

As you read this book, I pray you are inspired to believe the incredible, see the invisible, and do the impossible. That you will be encouraged, strengthened and find hope in God's Word to transform your life beyond your dreams! I also pray that as you look into the Word of God it will feed your faith and starve your doubts. Regardless of the obstacles you are facing today, I want you to rest in the fact that this is not the end for you, but your best awaits you on the other side of ***your*** story!

Donald E. Battle

As a young boy, I remember playing with tadpoles in the ditch in front of the projects where I lived. One day, curiosity got the best of me, and I decided to walk across the ditch to see what was on the other side. To my amazement, there was a whole new world across the tracks which was far different from the neighborhood where I lived. The homes were beautiful with well-manicured lawns and the look of affluence was everywhere. What I saw spoke of status and wealth. Right then and there something ignited in me that there was a better way of living, and I deserved to live just as good.

Sometimes our vision can be limited to the place of our surroundings. As a child, I had become so accustomed to the living conditions of being raised in the projects. But my expectation that there was more in life for me to experience didn't come alive until I saw something better. What if I had not taken that seemingly insignificant path to the other side?

I can ask you the same question, why haven't you crossed the ditch in your life? This place can represent something different for everyone. My ditch was the projects and being raised in a single-parent household. Your ditch may be fear, low self-esteem, failure or abuse. It is the thing that presents a barrier between where you are and where God has ultimately called you to go. How long will you allow your current situation to be a ceiling on how far you can go in life?

The purpose of a ditch is to be a place for runoff water to flow so the highway doesn't flood. There may be some things you need to let runoff from your life. We can often find our lives so flooded with problems and issues that we hydroplane off the path we're supposed to be taking to our place called "there."

Many of you have not only found yourselves in the ditch of life, but you have set up home. I Peter 5:7 (AMPC) reminds us to do the following, *"Casting the whole of your care [all your anxieties, all your worries, all your concerns, once and for all] on Him..."*

Let those things from the past runoff into the ditch. It's time for you to gain momentum in the plan of God for your life. You are never limited to where you are or where you've been. When you look through the eyes of who you are in Christ, just know that with God nothing is impossible.

Faith to Believe

Several years ago, on one of my trips to Haiti, I met a young man named Bildad. He and his friend were drawn to our group. We watched as they would jump on the back of Tap Taps (privately owned vans, pick-up trucks or buses used to serve as taxis in Haiti) and travel around the city. These young men have never left their country, but the more they spent time with us, the more they expressed a growing desire to come to America. We decided to have them come for a visit and just about that time Haiti experienced a massive earthquake.

Bildad and his friend applied for a Visa and were denied. But they did not give up. In their hearts this was just a delay. So, they got two chairs, sat in the chairs, extended their arms and simulated their plane ride to America! They were convinced that one day their dream would become a reality and they did not lose hope. They got their Visas, came to America and stayed at our home.

One day I preached a message entitled "You Ain't Seen Nothing Yet!" And Bildad grabbed hold of that word. God miraculously moved and opened a door for him to stay with a family in Tennessee and they put him in school.

About two years ago, he showed up at my house with a new car and a Bachelor's degree and told me, "Bishop, you ain't seen nothing yet!" He has since returned to Haiti and has opened a school with 200 students currently enrolled. And most recently he has opened a restaurant. Won't God do it? But you must believe!

Bildad did not just sit there and wallow 'poor me, I'm stuck here in Haiti.' He got up, put action to his faith and did something. Every time I speak with him, he tells me "Bishop, you ain't seen nothing yet!"

It's time to stop crying over past seasons of disappointments and failures. Maybe you're not where you thought you would be at this stage in your life, but if you keep rehearsing what happened yesterday you'll miss what is destined for today. Lamentation 3:22-23 reminds us that God's mercies are new every morning. Every day that you are alive, God is giving you another chance to skip to the next track on your album of life.

You must start at the place of your faith. To leave the familiar for what is unknown, it requires faith. When God first spoke to Abram, His instructions were to *"Get thee out of thy country, and from thy kindred, and from thy father's house, unto a land that I will shew thee"* (Genesis 12:1). Abram had to first be willing to leave what was comfortable to pursue the greater things God had destined for him.

Our five senses are necessary to function in the natural realm; however, they limit our spiritual capacity to progress in God. Stepping out in faith requires a belief far greater than what we can see, touch, taste, feel and hear. Faith is not necessarily required as we experience life in our day to day interactions, but our ability to see things from a spiritual perspective requires that we walk by faith and not by sight (See II Corinthians 5:7).

Jesus shared this powerful spiritual truth with a doubting Thomas after His resurrection:

> *…Reach hither thy finger, and behold my hands; and reach hither thy hand, and thrust it into my side: and be not faithless, but believing…Thomas, because thou hast seen me, thou hast believed: blessed are they that have not seen, and yet have believed* (John 20:27-29).

Thomas had previously said he would only believe that Jesus rose from the dead if Jesus proved it to him by allowing him to use his sense of touch and place his hand on the wounds. But when Jesus showed up and offered to grant his request, Thomas was shocked and cried out: *"My Lord and my God"* (John 20:28).

Could it be possible that if Thomas did not see Jesus' wounds with his own eyes and touched it with his own hands, that he would have separated from his faith? Thomas started out doubting but became a believer. This encounter brought change to his life.

Kingdom Authority

As children of God, we should never forget that we have authority. That Jesus is the Source and giver of the authority we possess, and "the gates of hell cannot prevail against it."

> *And Jesus came and spake unto them (His disciples), saying, All power is given unto me in heaven and in earth. Go ye therefore, and teach all nations, baptizing them in the name of the Father, and of the Son, and of the Holy Ghost: Teaching them to observe all things whatsoever I have commanded you: and, lo, I am with you always, even unto the end of the world. Amen (Matthew 28:18-20).*

And they were astonished at his doctrine: for he taught them as one that had authority, and not as the scribes (Mark 1:22).

And when he had called unto him his twelve disciples, he gave them power against unclean spirits, to cast them out, and to heal all manner of sickness and all manner of disease (Matthew 10:1).

We have authority to command our blessings - to call the things that are not as though they are. We have been given authority to "cast out unclean spirits, to heal the sick and all manner of disease." Yes, "as it is in Heaven, so on earth." We are empowered to bind and loose on earth what is bound and loosed in Heaven. (See Matthew 18:18)

Jesus shared many things with His disciples just before His death. One of the things He told them was:

"I no longer call you servants, because a servant does not know his master's business. Instead, I have called you friends, for everything that I learned from my Father I have made known to you. You did not choose me, but I chose you and appointed you so that you might go and bear fruit—fruit that will last—and so that whatever you ask in my name the Father will give you. This is my command: Love each other" (John 15:15-16).

Remember, Jesus defeated our enemy more than 2000 years ago when He died and rose from the dead. He gave us kingdom authority...use it for His glory!!

> *Behold, I give unto you power to tread on serpents and scorpions, and over all the power of the enemy: and nothing shall by any means hurt you* (Luke 10:19).

This scripture tells us that we have been given authority over the enemy. Jesus did not leave us destitute and void of access to His power and ability to resist the attacks of our adversary. The same power that raised Christ from the dead dwells within us. The Greater One (the Holy Spirit) was sent from God the Father into the earth to empower believers to live in complete victory and to execute Kingdom business.

If Jesus has given us authority over the enemy, then why are we so afraid of what the devil can do to us? As followers of Christ it does not mean we won't experience fear, but the Word of God tells us that "there is no fear in love. But perfect love drives out fear, because fear has to do with punishment. The one who fears is not made perfect in love." (1 John 4:18). Fear is a spirit that is not from God, and we must not allow it to control our lives in any form.

Don't fool yourself, we have an enemy called the devil and his goal is to kill, steal and destroy. In the Bible he is called the "accuser of the brethren" (Revelation 12:10), who goes around *like* a roaring lion, seeking whom he may devour" (1 Peter 5:8). The devil is a liar, and the father of lies. But don't forget he has been defeated by Jesus Christ our Lord (See Colossians 2:15), and greater is he that is in you, than he that is in the world…" (1 John 4:4)

If we only recognized the power within us, we would never walk in fear. The only power the devil has over the child of God is what we permit him. *"Submit yourselves therefore to God. Resist the devil, and he will flee from you"* (James 4:7). The Holy Spirit living and working through you and me is greater than any force of the enemy.

We must stand our ground and live in accordance with our belief in God's might. We must affirm the power and protection of God over our lives, our families and our nation each and every day.

Throughout his lifetime, the psalmist David endured many afflictions. Saul relentlessly pursued him with intent to kill him, and, at one point, David's spirit was exceedingly sorrowful and depressed. He suffered reproach, was exiled, and had to overcome the guilt and shame of his sins. However, David found hope in God who delivered him, and declared in Psalm 27:

> *The Lord is my light and my salvation; whom shall I fear? the Lord is the strength of my life; of whom shall I be afraid? When the wicked, even mine enemies and my foes, came upon me to eat up my flesh, they stumbled and fell. Though an host should encamp against me, my heart shall not fear: though war should rise against me, in this will I be confident* (Psalm 27:1-3).

David understood that God's power was greater than the evil forces attacking his mind; therefore, he placed his trust and faith solely in God. While good relationships are important, there are some problems our friends and family simply cannot solve. Only the power of Christ can lead us to victory when we are under spiritual attack. It takes a divine power to nullify the evil designed to destroy us.

See Yourself Blessed

When you take God at His Word and see yourself blessed instead of cursed, you become a magnet for attracting the blessings of the Lord.

> *But thou shalt remember the Lord thy God: for it is he that giveth thee power to get wealth, that he may establish his covenant…* (Deuteronomy 8:18).

The Bible also teaches us that *"…as he thinketh in his heart, so is he…"* (Proverbs 23:7). Your thoughts determine the direction and course for your life. Your actions are simply a byproduct of your most dominant thoughts. First, we think and then we respond. As you meditate on the Word, you renew your mind to what rightfully belongs to you through redemption. The same blessing that rested on Abraham has been bestowed upon those who are in Christ Jesus (See Galatians 3:14). We are the spiritual seed of Abraham and receive the blessing as our divine inheritance.

God's Blessing Cannot Be Reversed

In the book of Numbers, Chapters 22 and 23, we read the story of Balak, the king of Moab, who was envious of God's favor upon the nation of Israel. He attempted to bribe the prophet Balaam with riches if he would pronounce a curse upon the people of God. For a moment, Balaam considered the king's request and made his petition before the altar of God.

> *And the LORD put a word in Balaam's mouth, and said, Return unto Balak, and thus thou shalt speak. And he returned unto him, and, lo, he stood by his burnt sacrifice, he, and all the princes of Moab. And he took up his parable, and said, Balak the king of Moab hath brought me from Aram, out of the mountains of the east, saying, Come, curse me Jacob, and come, defy Israel. How shall I curse, whom God hath not cursed? or how shall I defy, whom the LORD hath not defied? For from the top of the rocks I see him, and from the hills I behold him: lo, the people shall dwell alone, and shall not be reckoned among the nation* (Numbers 23:5-9).

Despite continuous pressure from the king, the word of the Lord to the prophet was only to bless Israel. Notice the prophet's response to the king:

> *God is not a man, that he should lie; neither the son of man, that he should repent: hath he said, and shall he not do it? or hath he spoken, and shall he not make it good? Behold, I have received commandment to bless: and he hath blessed; and I cannot reverse it* (Numbers 23:19-20).

God is not a respecter of persons. Not even kings and queens can undo God's blessings. If He says you are blessed, then you are blessed. He is not a man that He should lie. The same way He blessed Israel is the same blessing that's available to every born-again believer today. Ephesians 1:3 reminds us that we have been blessed with EVERY spiritual blessing in the heavenlies. It doesn't matter what plot the enemy has planned against you; it's not greater than the blessing God has pronounced upon you. Every morning when you open your eyes you should confess, "the blessing of God is working for me, protecting me in every way, making provisions for my every need, and guarding me against all evil."

When your faith is firmly planted in what God has said concerning you, your resolve becomes unbreakable. That's why David said, *"I will bless the Lord at all times: his praise shall continually be in my mouth"* (Psalm 34:1). David refused to be moved because he knew God to be greater than the obstacles he faced.

We must never forget that God wants His children blessed beyond measure. But you have to believe it to receive it! According to Psalm 115:14, *"The Lord shall increase you more and more, you and your children."* Therefore, you have to take God at His Word and 'see' your blessings – see your bills paid, even to the point of having your debts wiped clean, your health intact and your needs met in every way to the full and overflow!

Now to Him who is able to [carry out His purpose and] do superabundantly more than all that we dare ask or think [infinitely beyond our greatest prayers, hopes, or dreams], according to His power that is at work within us, [21] *to Him be the glory in the church and in Christ Jesus throughout all generations forever and ever. Amen* (Ephesians 3:20-21).

Truly, what God has for you is so vast, so big – it cannot be measured. *"You prepare a table before me in the presence of my enemies; You anoint my head with oil; My cup runs over"* (Psalm 23: 5). God wants to bless you to the point your cup runs over, so you will know the blessing is not just for you but that you are indeed blessed to be a blessing! Believe God. Take Him at His Word. Release yourself from a closed mindset.

Sometimes we believe we can only receive when God's Word comes from "someone special." I know from personal experience. I remember the time I was at TBN waiting backstage for the program to begin and was looking for my favorite egg sandwich.

I loved the sandwiches they served before you go on stage. The egg salad sandwich was my favorite, but that night they were finished. As I was looking around, the lady who usually served the refreshments walked into the room. She turned to me and said: "The Lord told me to give you a word," to which I responded: "With all those great preachers out there, the Lord told *you* to give *me* a word?" I asked her "Lady, where's the egg salad sandwich?"

You see, sometimes we think only the preacher can have a word for us. Often God is trying to get a word to you, but you think it can only come from a certain source. Here I was thinking of all my accomplishments swirling around in my head, like 20 plus years in ministry, multiple campuses, thousands of members and this sandwich serving lady is telling me she has a word for me. "Yes," she said, "Exodus 34:10." I looked at her and then I decided to look up the scripture. I found it and the Word of God to me said, "**God is going to do something in your life that has never been done before.**" That word had such a powerful impact on my life...it was a wow moment! You have to believe that if God says He is going to do something in your life that He will do just what He says.

Don't get so high minded you cannot be open and receptive to what God says, because God can use any vessel He chooses to accomplish His purpose.

In 2 Kings Chapter 4, we read the story of a woman whose husband had died and she went to the prophet Elisha and told him: "Your servant my husband is dead, and you know that he revered the Lord. But now his creditor is coming to take my two boys as his slaves."

Elisha responded to her by asking, "How can I help you? "What do you have in your house?" to which she replied, "I have nothing at all, except a small jar of oil." The man of God gave her specific instructions to "go ask all her neighbors for empty jars. Don't ask for just a few," he said, "get lots! And when you are through collecting, go inside your house and shut the door behind you and your sons and pour oil into all the jars, and as you fill each jar, put it to the side."

Of course, that kind of talk did not seem to make a lot of sense to her, but she was obedient, and did exactly as she was told: she got the jars, went back to her house, shut the door behind her and poured the oil until every single vessel was filled. When all the jars were full, she asked her son to "Bring me another one." He told her, "Mama, there is not a jar left." And immediately the oil stopped flowing. She then went and told the man of God what happened and he instructed her to "Go, sell the oil, pay off your debts and you and your sons can live on what is left."

Here we see clearly that this woman reached out to the man of God hoping he would do something for her, to help her out of her predicament, not realizing that what she needed was already in her house...she just didn't know it.

For some of you looking at what you are dealing with right now, it is hard to conceive or even believe you already have what you need to get out of a difficult situation. That financial breakthrough you so need, that new car, the new house, the healing, salvation of your children and loved ones, that business you so want to get off the ground, and so much more, it is already in your house!

There are many people dealing with health issues right now. It may be you or a loved one, but you have to see yourself healthy and healed in spite of what you feel. Your God wants the best of health for you.

"Beloved, I wish above all things that thou mayest prosper and be in health, even as thy soul prospereth" (3 John 1:2).

Based on your finances, you may be surrounded by lack, more month than money, behind on all your bills, but you have to believe God that wealth is coming your way, and encourage yourself in the Lord and know that your God shall supply all of your needs according to His riches in glory by Christ Jesus (See Philippians 4:19).

Your worst experience is right next door to the best days in your life. The Psalmist David in 1 Samuel 26 and 27 had some dark days in Ziklag, some days when he may have thought the sun would not shine anymore, but he kept on moving, he kept on trusting, he kept on believing all the way from the cave to the splendor of living in the palace in Zion.

Your Ziklag experience is right next door to your Zion. You have to purpose in your heart that you won't quit, you won't give up, but you are going to "pursue, overtake and recover all." We are rightly told to "Never despise the days of small beginnings" (Zechariah 4:10).

It won't be long before what you need to turn your situation around is here, so you can go from what has been...from "What is this?" to "Can This Be?" The day of your Amos 9:13 blessing is coming your way, "It really won't be long now!" See it, believe it and you will take hold of the good things God has for you.

"Yes indeed, it won't be long now." God's Decree. Things are going to happen so fast your head will swim, one thing fast on the heels of the other. You won't be able to keep up. Everything will be happening at once—and everywhere you look, blessings! Blessings like wine pouring off the mountains and hills. I'll make everything right again for my people Israel: "They'll rebuild their ruined cities. They'll plant vineyards and drink good wine. They'll work their gardens and eat fresh vegetables. And I'll plant them, plant them on their own land. They'll never again be uprooted from the land I've given them." God, your God, says so (Amos 9:13).

Up for The Challenge

Life is full of challenges and often when we are faced with difficulties, we feel like we are all alone. Jesus tells us *"In this godless world you will continue to experience difficulties. But take heart! I've conquered the world"* (John 16:33).

We must not allow our feelings to control how we respond to difficulties. I have found that some of my greatest accomplishments were achieved during times of great challenge. When it seemed like nothing was going right in the natural, God would supernaturally come through for me because my faith in Him never faltered. The Word tells us, "… *let us not be weary in well doing: for in due season we shall reap, if we faint not*" (Galatians 6:9).

God has placed victory on the inside of you; therefore, defeat is not a part of your future. You are a winner. You are more than a conqueror.

One of the things that makes a basketball player great is his ability to predict his opponent's moves. When a player is moving down the court, his opponents are looking for opportunity to see where they can steal the ball. The devil operates in quite the same manner. It may seem like something is coming your way, but remember he is always on the lookout to see how and what he can steal from you. He is a liar from the beginning of time and always will be.

I'm reminded of the time when Gwen and I were getting ready to expand back in 2002. We knew we had God's Word on our move, but we were financially challenged. For a year we lived on the north side of Atlanta. We didn't let anyone know we had moved, and especially where we had moved to. Of course, time and time again we would run into people up north and they would ask, "What are you doing up here?" This was somewhat awkward, so I would mumble and pretend I had reason to be there. Eventually, I came to the conclusion that God is God all by Himself and He promised to work all things in my favor and according to His purpose, including this move. I knew this did not just happen by chance, but God had ordained it and if this was a challenge, I was ready for it.

I do understand that there are times when it is okay to wait in the wings for just a right moment, but I have also come to understand that in God's perfect time there is no holding back when it's your time to step out. You may think that stepping out is the biggest mistake of your life, but I believe it's about to become your greatest miracle. When challenges come your way, look to God and see brighter days ahead.

See Opportunities Not Problems

In every problem situation there is an opportunity or a possibility to learn, grow and improve, but you have to see it before it manifests. In the story of Joshua, Caleb and the ten other spies, they all saw the same things when they spied out the Promised Land. But they came to different conclusions. Joshua and Caleb saw opportunities and possibilities, while their ten buddies saw nothing but problems. Why? Because they viewed the matter from a different perspective.

Even though the ten spies saw the things promised to them by God, they were of the mindset that there were more obstacles and problems in their way that would hinder the good things they wanted and could have. In the end, they returned to their leader with a bad report, concluding the enemy was bigger and more powerful. They saw the enemy as giants and more superior and viewed themselves as mere grasshoppers, inferior and incapable of walking in victory.

But thank God for Joshua and Caleb. They were now standing on the ground in the land flowing with milk and honey. The Promised Land. Not only did they want what they saw, they believed they were well able to possess it. Did they see the same things the others saw? Yes, they did but they refused to walk in fear and unbelief. Instead they stood firm in faith knowing their God was bigger than all the obvious barriers staring them in the face.

As a pastor, I see people all the time who want the good things God has promised. They confess they want strong families, they want children walking the godly path. They want God's blessings on their marriage, their health, their finances. Yes, they want these blessings but are not willing to go after it – not willing to pursue what God says they can have and quickly or easily give up at the first sign of a problem or a setback. Like the ten spies, that is not pleasing to God. If we are going to achieve success, we cannot accept defeat.

Listen out for Your Victory

In the second book of Kings, there was an event when Ben-Hadad, King of Syria, sent a great army of horses and chariots to the city of Dothan. They were sent at night to the prophet Elisha's home to prevent his escape. Elisha's servant got up early in the morning, and when he saw the warriors surrounding the city, he rushed to tell Elisha (See II King 6:8-18). He was probably afraid when he saw all that, but Elisha was not moved by what was happening, he simply said, "...*Fear not: for they that be with us are more than they that be with them*" (II Kings 6:16).

> *And Elisha prayed, and said, Lord, I pray thee, open his eyes, that he may see. And the Lord opened the eyes of the young man; and he saw: and behold, the mountain was full of horses and chariots of fire round about Elisha. And when they came down to him, Elisha prayed unto the Lord, and said, Smite this people, I pray thee, with blindness. And he smote them with blindness according to the word of Elisha* (II Kings 6:17-18).

Elisha's servant could not initially see God's divine protection. In his mind, he may have thought this was a hopeless situation, but he did not truly know the God of Elisha! Likewise, you and I need to open our eyes and see the extent of God's protection over us. Even though the enemy is plotting against your every move, you must know that God has something better waiting for you. You may be assaulted on every side but know that you are called to walk in victory. You've got to get joy in your spirit, and give God praise in the midst of a situation that may look hopeless.

When the children of Israel were faced with the wall at Jericho, they did exactly what God told them to do and walked in victory.

No matter how looming your "wall" may seem today, it can and will come down if you do what God tells you to do. All you need is a word from the Lord! It is amazing the marvelous results you can have when you see your challenge as an opportunity for God to show up and show out, so you can do your victory dance!

It is important to understand that God's will for you is that the walls in your life must come down. You must never allow life's walls to bear down on you or to keep you blocked in places that the enemy wants to keep you trapped.

Regardless of how great the attack, we can rejoice that in this battle, we have what we need.

Rise in the Face of Attacks

The Apostle Paul was a servant of God who experienced many trials in his lifetime. He was whipped, beaten with rods, stoned, shipwrecked, robbed, persecuted and falsely accused, but he maintained a positive outlook that the results would be greater than the trials.

"But we have this treasure in earthen vessels, that the excellency of the power may be of God, and not of us" (II Corinthians 4:7). What is this treasure in earthen vessels? It's our faith and implicit trust in God's Word. Our faith causes us to rise in the face of the enemy's attacks:

> *We are troubled on every side, yet not distressed; we are perplexed, but not in despair; persecuted, but not forsaken; cast down, but not destroyed; Always bearing about in the body the dying of the Lord Jesus, that the life also of Jesus might be made manifest in our body. For we which live are always delivered unto death for Jesus' sake, that the life also of Jesus might be made manifest in our mortal flesh* (II Corinthians 4:8-11).

Our faith gives us the strength to persevere. Just as Jesus rose from the grave, we will rise out of our troubles. Do not give up. Paul delivered this powerful message of hope when he said:

> *For which cause we faint not; but though our outward man perish, yet the inward man is renewed day by day. For our light affliction, which is but for a moment, worketh for us a far more exceeding and eternal weight of glory; while we look not at the things which are seen, but at the things which are not seen: for the things which are seen are temporal; but the things which are not seen are eternal* (II Corinthians 4:16-18).

While you are standing in faith, don't be too quick to share your vision or your problems with everybody. Unfortunately, not everyone wishes you well or wants you to succeed. It may seem only natural to share some good news about your plans, vision and aspirations, but you also don't need others speaking negatively over what God has ordained for your life.

Keep your attention focused on God. It has been said, "Never let the devil see you sweat." The enemy can and will use what you say against you. Your words are either going to give access for heaven to manifest on your behalf or for the enemy to wreak havoc in your life.

Only God is omniscient. Therefore, the enemy doesn't know what is happening in you, unless you blurt it out! He can only find out if you choose to share it through the words of your mouth. Negative words open the door for evil results, so when you confess your fears, you give the enemy ammunition to work against you. Never give your adversary opportunity to confront you at your weakest point. Don't ever forget that a lot is at stake in the words you say. *"Death and life are in the power of the tongue, and those who love it will eat its fruit"* (Proverbs 18:21). Speak God's Word.

Choose Your Words Carefully

Stop rehearsing your problems. It amazes me how some people can't wait to be asked, "How are you doing?" That simple question gives them the perfect opportunity to grab a listening ear to complain: "Nobody knows the trouble I see, only Jesus." Do you know that as you seek sympathy, your flesh is telling you, "Feed me. Feed me. I want you to feel how I feel. Come on, share in my misery with me." On the other hand, your spirit is saying, "Shut up and pull yourself together because the Word about you is true." You should listen to the Spirit of God and claim your victory. Remember Joshua 6:2? God did not say that He was going to or might give Joshua Jericho. It was already done. God told Joshua, "I have already given you Jericho." They had what they needed. Joshua received God's Word and he spoke it, *"Joshua said unto the people, Shout; for the Lord hath given you the city"* (Joshua 6:16).

Am I saying that disclosing your issues or concerns with a trusted friend or counselor is wrong? No, not at all. As a matter of fact, it can sometimes be good therapy, but there is a time and a place for everything. To always be talking about your troubles is the sign of a greater problem. You will cement the pain associated with the burden in your spirit when you continuously rehearse it rather than focus on the solution. Instead of claiming ownership of the hurt, affirm God's promise to restore what has been broken.

I've learned to talk less and read the Word of God more. The result is that my spirit is strengthened, and I am better equipped to deal with any situation. Instead of allowing the enemy to agitate me into speaking excessively or acting in the flesh, I've learned to stand still and see God at work.

Sometimes, we may want to express our feelings and have our voices heard, but we would do good to follow the instructions outlined in James 1:19: *"Wherefore, my beloved brethren, let every man be swift to hear, slow to speak, slow to wrath."*

Selecting Your Circle

We see in the Bible that wherever Jesus went, people came to hear His teaching, but not everyone who heard Him teach followed Him or did what He said. Likewise, not everyone that followed Him became His disciple. And when you look at those who were His disciples, you see that Jesus had an inner circle of people He spent more time with and in whom He invested the most.

"After six days Jesus took Peter, James and John with him and led them up a high mountain, where they were all alone. There he was transfigured before them" (Mark 9:2). As God's children, we should always strive to be like Jesus. Therefore, we should be particular in choosing who we spend the most time with and who we invest most of our lives into.

It is true that if you are going to accomplish great things in life, you cannot do it by yourself nor can you do it with negative or unproductive people. You need individuals around you who will bring out the best in you. Not pretenders, but people who truly love you, people who believe in you and who will go the extra mile to help you fulfill your goals and dreams and walk in your destiny.

By saying that, it does not mean you cannot have relationship with all kinds of people, it simply means you cannot let everyone into your inner circle. Ask God for wisdom in determining your core group, people you can be totally open and honest with, whether family, friend, church or the marketplace. Remember, the people you put in your inner circle may not necessarily know everything, but they should be folks who will encourage you, tell you the truth and push you in the right direction.

Never forget, when you are about to birth a promise God has given you, His Spirit will quicken you and, like Elizabeth, cause your 'baby to leap.' When you are connected to the right people in life, it should bear witness that this is the right place to be. It is true that we can at times find ourselves in the right place, but with the wrong people. I refuse to enter fellowship with folks who don't motivate me to aspire to greater things. You must distance yourself from the company of those who make you feel like you're about to wither away in defeat and surround yourself with people of vision.

Stop associating with dream killers and thieves. They are everywhere! You may find them in your home or at your place of work. You may even find them at church!

You must choose wisely who you allow in your circle of influence. They can help you build and achieve your goals, or they can ruin them. The traits of dream killers and thieves are easy to identify:

- **The Know-It-All**: They tend to think they know everything. Sometimes they assert that they know more about you and your capabilities than you know yourself!

- **The Spoiler**: Every time you share your plans, they

will find a reason why your initiatives will not bear fruit, or why you shouldn't even try!

- **The Negative Nancy**: These people express negativity about ideas, especially yours. They are eager to recall all the failures of your past.

- **The Cynic**: After failure, these people are quick to tell you, "I told you so."

- **The Pretender**: They make you believe they are on your side when they are not.

It is important that you assess the people around you. Be mindful that everyone who advises you in a manner which you dislike is not a dream killer and thief, but you should check for patterns. If a person consistently displays the traits I've identified above, it may be time to purge them from your life. Ask God for discernment to bring the right people into your life.

It's important to remember that dream killers and thieves are not always people. Our emotions and actions can also kill our ambition. Procrastination, fear, worry, anxiety, resentment, and anger can all distract you from reaching your goals and living the abundant life God has promised you.

Strong Vision Is Required

Ask God for strong vision. With strong vision, you can maximize your assets. Most of us don't understand this principle because we focus on our weaknesses rather than our strengths. Once you maximize your strengths, you will leave the enemy speechless! The devil may know how to push and prod you, but you are not influenced by him. We can be perplexed but not distressed, cast down but not destroyed. When you stand up in the strength of Christ, nothing, absolutely nothing, can stop you.

Paul was a man who learned to be resolute in the face of adversity. In the book of Acts, the enemy stirred up a tempest to cause the ship that Paul was on to be tossed about by the waves (See Acts 27:1-44). That storm raged for fourteen days, and it looked like no one would survive. Great fear and desperation came upon the passengers and crew, but Paul stood and declared what he heard from God:

> *And now I exhort you to be of good cheer: for there shall be no loss of any man's life among you, but of the ship. For there stood by me this night the angel of God, whose I am, and whom I serve, saying, Fear not, Paul; thou must be brought before Caesar: and, lo, God hath given thee all them that sail with thee. Wherefore, sirs, be of good cheer: for I believe God, that it shall be even as it was told to me* (Acts 27:22-25).

Just as the Word of God indicated, the boat was wrecked at the final stretch, but its crew swam to a nearby island to safety. Even in a storm, you can reach for your breakthrough. But I need to ask you, how badly do you want it? It is not going to just fall into your lap – it will take some effort on your part. Yes, to have something you have never had, you have to do something you have never done. Is God making you work for it? No, but there are situations and obstacles in your way that won't make it easy for you, so you will have to break through the pain, the fear, the doubt and know that with God all things are possible and that you possess the tools for warfare.

Remain in your 'boat' until the time appointed by God. This is the 'boat' to your destiny, ministry and calling. Yes, bad things may happen to you while you are on board but remain steadfast and God will see you through. The tempest may rage against you. All hell may break loose. Things may not turn out the way you want, but don't abandon ship. Stay on board until you hear God speak. Then and only then are you to move in the direction He tells you.

At times, we can become so discouraged that we want to surrender; there are voices in our heads encouraging us to quit. The boat appears to be sinking, and no one is around to save us. The enemy says you will only last a couple more months, weeks or even days. If you consider this instead of the promises of God, you may surrender to the enemy's lie.

Believe me, the devil is betting on you to tap out. He wants you to jump ship and leave God's presence. Be warned that if you vacate God's presence, you will NOT survive. Life will overpower and overwhelm you, and you will drown in the ocean of regret, sorrow, worry, and guilt. Victory says that is not God's design for you.

In the face of every situation, you must stand your ground. Resist the temptation to do otherwise. Never allow the attacks or insults of people to cause you to abandon your calling. Likewise, don't let slanderous and false accusations tear your family apart. You must continuously pray for your children if it appears they are headed in the wrong direction. God promises that if you hold on, He will supply your every need. Through God and His Word, you have authority over the enemy.

Paul said, *"Always bearing about in the body the dying of the Lord Jesus, that the life also of Jesus might be made manifest in our body"* (II Corinthians 4:10). Paul compares the sufferings of other Christians and himself to those of the Lord Jesus Christ. It would be naïve for any Christian to believe they are exempt from suffering in this life.

The people of God have always suffered. It is part of being a Christian. Though we may be cast down and forsaken by those around us, God will never withdraw His presence from our lives. It is in Him that we live and move and have our being (See Acts 17:28). The Holy Spirit lives in us and is our salvation. Through the Holy Spirit, we have inside information and know things before they happen.

We must never forget that the Holy Spirit is our Helper (See John 14:26). Therefore, we will not fear. Jesus said, *"But when He, the Spirit of truth comes, He will guide you into all the truth..."* (John 16:13 NIV). It is important to learn to be led by the Holy Spirit to do what He tells you to do in every area of your life.

Pray in the Spirit

Praying in the Holy Spirit is a powerful tool for calling down Heaven's resources. When I'm praying in my heavenly language, it's my direct communication with the Most High God. And God responds to my needs with His arsenal. The Bible states that we do not know what we should pray, but the Spirit Himself intercedes for us (See Romans 8:26-27).

A lot of things happen that we don't understand because we are not in tune with God's Spirit, nor are we sufficiently attuned to pick up on things happening in the realm of the spirit. We are essentially spiritual beings with a soul (mind, will and emotions) housed within a physical body. Therefore, in 3 John 2, John prayed for prosperity and health for Gaius, even as his mind and emotions prospered.

In Romans 12:2, we are exhorted to be transformed by the renewing of our minds so that we may prove God's perfect will. When we have renewed our minds, nothing will stand in the way of our destiny. We will rid ourselves of small-mindedness and put aside the victim mentality. Ultimately, we will see ourselves as Christ sees us.

Power of the Word

It is true that the words we say and hear carry a lot of

weight. Therefore, it is vital to pay close attention to the words we speak, because words matter and carry more weight than you might think! At the start of your day, I challenge you to plant the seed of God's Word in your life by waking up each morning and speaking it over your day. Know that words are the tools God used in Creation, and His Word is powerful over every situation.

We know the power of the Word, because *"the worlds were framed by the word of God"* (Hebrews 11:13).

God said, "Let there be ..." and so it was (See Genesis 1:1-28). God uses words to bring light into darkness, to create or to destroy, to oppress or set free. Words are significant no matter how simple they may seem.

> *Even as Abraham believed God, and it was accounted to him for righteousness* (Galatians 3:6).
>
> *(As it is written, I have made thee a father of many nations,) before him whom he believed, even God, who quickeneth the dead, and calleth those things which be not as though they were* (Romans 4:17).

Abraham was considered righteous not because of his good deeds, but because he was faithful and believed in God's promises. Abraham acted on his faith and agreed with God when He called things that were not as though they already were.

This agreement meant that Abraham believed he would have a son from Sarah even though they were both well past their childbearing years. Abraham spoke the same words that God spoke and declared himself father of many nations!

You can take the promises of God and declare that you are wealthy. Speak the Word that wealth and riches are in your house. Declare that your household will be saved by the blood of Christ, and that no weapon formed against you shall prosper!

We can also declare with Paul, *"For which cause we faint not; but though our outward man perish, yet the inward man is renewed day by day"* (2 Corinthians 4:16).

Seek God in Your Crisis

Sometimes we find ourselves in situations that seem like life is spinning out of control and we can hardly catch our breath. What do you do? When you are in a crisis, seek God and thank Him for the solution. If you can't come up with the right words, pray in the Holy Spirit until you feel peace and then go to sleep. By the time you wake up, you should sense that God has already started to work in your favor. Your spirit has overcome your flesh, and now you can see things clearly. Your adversary foolishly thought he was going to confuse you enough to derail what God has in store for you, but he didn't count on you increasing your strength through prayer.

It is important to daily exercise self-control and wisdom. Do not allow your peace and joy to be interrupted, thereby placing you in a state of panic and distress where you would run to your friends and family for assistance. You choose to obey God and trust Him to solve your problems.

You must decide to not lean on human strength, wisdom, understanding, wealth or positions, but to trust God all the way, no matter what. *"Some trust in chariots, and some in horses: but we will remember the name of the Lord our God"* (Psalm 20:7).

When you put the Word of God into action and you have matured enough, then you can declare that every tongue which rises against you in judgment will be condemned (See Isaiah 54:17). Putting God's Word into action is a privilege and right of God's children, and there is nothing the enemy can do about it.

God will deliver you out of your trial because He is always and forever true to His promises. Therefore, you can be assured you are not a victim, but a victor! Greater is He that is in me, than he that is in the world!

Many years ago, I watched the movie, *Seabiscuit*. It's a wonderful story of a race horse who conquers adversity. Throughout his career, Seabiscuit experienced numerous setbacks, but on his final race (his 3rd attempt) he was boxed in by one horse on each side. As the horses neared the end of the race, Seabiscuit pulled at his jockey's hands as if to say, "Let's do it!" Seabiscuit's jockey, Red Pollard, said a prayer.

A gap opened up and Red shouted, "Now, Pop!" Despite the blistering pace, Seabiscuit accelerated to the front. In the homestretch, Seabiscuit looked his competitor in the eye and sprinted ahead leaving him behind.

Seabiscuit's time was the second fastest run on an American track for that distance. "Don't think he didn't know he was the hero," Red said.

You may not feel like a hero now or that you have what it takes to succeed. You may not have suitable academic or professional qualifications for something you desire to do, or you may not have the right connections to secure a particular job. You may feel you were born on the wrong side of the tracks, and that this is the best you can do. To you I say, *never surrender! Stay your course!* It's not over until God says it's over!

God loves taking the last and making it first (See Matthew 20:16). He delights in the odds being stacked against you, so when He brings you out of your predicament He can get the glory.

When God blesses you at just the right time you will have no choice but to declare in amazement, *"If God be for us, who can be against us?"* (Romans 8:31).

> *For our light affliction, which is but for a moment, worketh for us a far more exceeding and eternal weight of glory; while we look not at the things which are seen, but at the things which are not seen: for the things which*

are seen are temporal; but the things which are not seen are eternal (II Corinthians 4:17-18).

The word temporal (as it relates to time) means "subject to change." The devil can only work his evil plan for a limited time; it's only temporary. After you have prayed and put on the whole armor of God, all that is left for you to do is STAND and see the salvation of the Lord.

While you're standing on the Word, you can laugh at the enemy! The book of Job says the devil goes "to and fro," which is a sign of restlessness. He is aware that his time will soon expire, and it makes him shudder to see you successfully resisting his attacks. Don't look at your circumstances because they will change. You were never destined to live in the valley of distress; it's time to move into your promised land.

Like Paul to the Philippians, *"but this one thing I do, forgetting those things which are behind, and reaching forth unto those things which are before, I press toward the mark for the prize of the high calling of God in Christ Jesus"* (Philippians 3:13-14). Go for it, your race has already been determined – you win because the Greater One is in you and if you can believe it today, He is already turning things around and something good is about to happen for you! Take God at His Word and know that what you need is already in you…yes, it's in the house!

Often when things go terribly wrong in our lives, we feel as if we are being "sifted" or tossed around. Who is responsible for that, and what do we do? I want to look at the lives of Job and other godly men as role models for us to study.

> *There was a man in the land of Uz, whose name was Job; and that man was perfect and upright, and one that feared God, and eschewed evil* (Job 1:1).

It's difficult to imagine anyone who is perfect and upright. Yet, the Bible tells us Job was faultless and honorable.

Now, some may ask, "By whose standards was he righteous?" He was upright with God because he was a God-fearing man.

Yes, Job was a clear example of an upright man. He is recorded as one who stood his ground and did not disobey God. Job feared God and respected His commandments even when life was tough, and he did not give in to the negative advice of his friends.

Job's case is a clarion call to all Christians. It is indicative of the fact that those who put their trust in the Lord will not be put to shame. What do you do when situations are unbearable? Do you renounce your faith and curse God? Your answer should be no. For God's grace is sufficient to lead you out of any troubling situation. Hence,

I urge you to anchor your faith in God and He will lift you up.

God showered Job with many blessings. He had seven sons, three daughters, and many servants. All his needs were provided by God. He had riches which included seven thousand sheep, three thousand camels, five hundred yoke of oxen and five hundred female asses. In all, he was adjudged as "the greatest man of the east!" (Job 1:3).

Although Job's suffering was great he did not respond to it with fear, but rather he chose to walk it out in faith. My question is: How will you respond to your storm when everything comes crashing down around you? With fear or with faith in God to see you through? I encourage you to choose faith. Remember, Job's pain was so intense, he ripped off his clothing, shaved his head and fell flat out on the ground. The children he loved, covered with prayer, made sacrifices for, were now all dead. Yet, in spite of all that, Job refused to sin by blaming God. It takes a man with faith in God to cry out in the midst of suffering and say:

> *Naked I came from my mother's womb, and naked I will depart. The Lord gave and the Lord has taken away; may the name of the Lord be praised* (Job 1:21).
>
> *Shall we accept good from God, and not trouble? In all this, Job did not sin in what he said* (Job 2:10).

When we choose to trust God and walk in faith, it doesn't mean we won't have problems. Yet through it all we can have confidence that God will never leave us nor forsake us. Jesus said, *"In this world you will have trouble. But take heart! I have overcome the world"* (John 16:33).

Well, is it even possible to have faith while surrounded by loss on every side? Yes, you can when you know in your heart it won't be like this always, a change has got to come. From tragedy and great loss, untold beauty can actually emerge.

As you read Job's amazing story, you see that although he chose the path of faith instead of fear, he had questions, lots of questions. I have been in many situations where I have asked God questions, like Why? or Why not? or even Why me? No doubt you have too. But you and I are no exception. The Bible is filled with characters who asked God questions. David asked many, such as: How long, O Lord? Will you forget me forever? How long will you hide your face from me? (See Psalm 13) Let us not forget that even Jesus, God's beloved Son asked: Father, is there another way out? (See Luke 22:42-43).

So often the things we go through in life doesn't make sense. Here is the same man whose story started out the picture of perfection, blameless in the eyes of God, beautiful healthy family, wealth beyond measure, then comes trouble and suffering crashing down like you have never seen.

It is true that trouble has no respect for persons. It doesn't matter who you are or where you come from, sooner or later, it is coming your way whether you like it or not. But you don't have to cave in. You can still choose to walk in faith in the midst of it all. Even with your best friends speaking negatively about you; your very wife or loved one recommending you "curse God and die!" Like Job, you can say, *"Though He slay me I will trust Him"* (Job 13:15). Believe me, faith will cast out fear!

Job's story was real and so is yours. So is your God. He is real, and He is in control of all things concerning you, even when it doesn't seem like it in your eyes. When it doesn't make sense to you, you can still have confidence that your turnaround is coming. It won't always be like this, your best days are yet ahead.

Like Job, you too can say, *"I know that my Redeemer lives, and that in the end he will stand upon the earth"* (Job 19:25). He will never leave you nor forsake you.

The same God who is with you when things are going good is the same God who will stand by your side on the not so good days. He will come through for you as He did for Job at the end of his story when Job got double for his trouble. There truly is another side to your story!

Fight Your Fears

Fear is something we must all overcome in life. It will try to paralyze and keep you from moving forward.

Unfortunately, fear of the unknown has caused many of us to give up on our dreams and miss great opportunities. Sometimes we even procrastinate by worrying, "What if this happens?" "What if it doesn't work out?" This is not what God wants for His children. The Bible says, *"For God hath not given us the spirit of fear; but of power, and of love, and of a sound mind"* (II Timothy 1:7). Living in fear keeps you in bondage. Claiming fear and speaking it into your life is destructive. You must fight your fears and overcome it because it is False Evidence Appearing Real.

God has given you the spiritual and mental capacity to overcome fear. It's time for you to move forward, step out in faith, and fulfill the purpose He has for you. You have the mind of Christ, and no weapon formed against you will prosper. No evil thoughts, worries, stress, feelings of guilt, and fear will overcome you when you stand in faith (See I Corinthians 2:16).

The Bible tells us a lot more about Job and his life. You see that his wonderful life was turned upside down when he lost everything. Nevertheless, He endured much suffering and in the end came out twice better than he was before. He never lost hope nor his faith in God. How will you respond to your storm when everything comes crashing down around you? I encourage you to choose faith.

Regardless of how bleak your circumstances are right now, God is holding you up. He is walking with you through the storms of life. You might be going through great challenges, and the pressures of life may be weighing you down. You may be crumbling under the weight of it all, but do not fear!

God is your refuge and strength. Lean on Him because there is no burden too heavy that He cannot bear and bring you into a place of total victory. He simply asks that you replace your fears and anxieties with faith, prayer, and praise. The peace of God, which fear tries to steal, will rest on you mightily.

> *Be careful for nothing; but in everything by prayer and supplication with thanksgiving let your requests be made known unto God. And the peace of God, which passeth all understanding, shall keep your hearts and minds through Christ Jesus* (Philippians 4:6-7).

We must move beyond fear and exercise our faith in God by making a decision to stay on track despite life's challenges.

Stay on Track

God will sometimes show me that I am doing the right thing even though things are not happening the way I expect. He reassures me that all is well, and that I am on the right path. He will say, "This is not where you need to be but you're on the right track." Such reassurance is important to me. To hear God speak reminds me that the steps of a righteous person are ordered by Him. It also shows that He is close to us and involved in our lives in the good and the bad times. He walks and talks with us and leads us as we allow Him.

It is true that we need God's wisdom and direction in every area of daily living if we are going to be successful in our deliberations. There are times when doubt and confusion will try to consume us by creating worry and anxiety. God's Word will make the difference by always encouraging us to move forward and remain steady and on track.

As you include God in every aspect of your life, He will show you the way. His Word says, *"And we know that all things work together for good to them that love God, to them who are the called according to his purpose"* (Romans 8:28). Don't you ever give up! But continue to follow His blueprint for your life and rest assured He will never abandon you.

If you ever feel like giving up, remember Joseph. He had a dream about his future greatness when he was seventeen years old. His dream was not fulfilled until several years later. During this time, he had to face many ups and downs while endeavoring to stay committed to serving God. His brothers threw him into a pit, and he was sold into slavery. Later while working in Potiphar's house, he was accused of raping his boss' wife and was thrown in prison and left there to rot. Those years he spent in the dark dungeons may have seemed endless, but God still had a plan for him. In the end, Joseph was victorious because he remained faithful to God.

Remember Moses? He was born to deliver the Israelites from Egypt. For forty years he lived in the desert tending sheep. At the appointed time, God appeared to him in the burning bush and told him to speak to Pharaoh about setting the Israelites free.

Moses and Joseph had to go through many trials before they received the promise of God. The things that happened to them did not make sense. Sometimes it can take months or even years before we see God's promises come to pass. We may start to doubt and feel that He has forsaken us, but I encourage you to not be sidetracked by the distractions or the distractors that come your way. Rather, you should focus on the promises of God and keep moving, looking to the author and finisher of your faith. In the end, you can only win.

Job had his distractors. His wife told him to curse God and die. In other words, she came to the conclusion that his life was no longer worth living. Can you imagine how heartbroken Job was when the woman he counted on for his greatest support told him he was better off dead?

Next, his friends came as distractors who had lost faith in Job as an upright man and accused him of sinning. As far as they were concerned, the only reason Job was in such calamity was because he had sinned. Instead of encouraging Job, they discouraged him. He had to draw from deep within and depend on his faith in God to come out on the winning side.

Oftentimes, the things we experience in life do not make sense. Trouble and suffering can come crashing into your life without warning. It doesn't matter who you are or where you come from, sooner or later it is coming your way whether you like it or not. However, you don't have to cave in and surrender. You can still choose to walk in faith in the midst of it all. Believe me, faith will cast out fear!

For a while, the devil can throw his worst punches at you. He can slander, accuse, and offend you in many ways. It's important to remember that even bad seasons have expiration dates. You will outlast him. Greater is God who lives in you than the devil and his cohorts (See I John 4:4). You aren't going to give up because you know he is a loser. Don't become weary in doing right. The Bible teaches that whatever a person sows, he will reap (See Galatians 6:7). It is a fact that God will not fail.

You may sometimes feel like living right is in vain. Just remember Job. Everyone saw the good life he had because of his right living. Imagine what others must have thought and said when calamity came his way. It's very likely they themselves wondered if it pays to be righteous. It seemed like Job's good had gone unnoticed, unappreciated and was a waste of time. But no, God sees everything, and He increased all that Job had by giving him double.

Likewise, God has not forgotten you. He has not abandoned His promises to bless and keep you in all your ways. You are going to rise up and be more than a conqueror through Him who loves you (See Roman 8:37). You may be battered and bruised by satan's relentless battles against you, but they cannot destroy you. God has given you mighty weapons to fight against the enemy (See Ephesians 6:11). His weapons are not carnal. In other words, they are not physical. You cannot rely on your intelligence, beauty, wealth, social status or any earthly possession to ward off the devil. Your strength comes from God.

The weapons of God will pull down the strongholds in your life: evil situations, bad habits, guilt, brokenness, wrong attitudes, and actions. The enemy's weapons are no match for your weapons in God! You are in a fight to the finish, and you will win. However, you cannot win this battle in your own strength but by submission to God and the power of the Holy Spirit. Use all the armor and weapons God has given you. Put on truth, righteousness, peace, faith, and salvation. Apply them to your life. Meditate on God's Word and pray fervently. Whatever you do, stay on track!

Rejoice in the Lord Always

Don't ever think that people are happy and content solely because of their material possessions. Ownership of cars, houses, and plots of land is no guarantee for inner happiness. The old adage says, "Never judge a book by its cover." Be careful not to judge people and situations by outward appearances.

God asked Samuel to anoint one of Jesse's sons to be king. Naturally, the prophet thought it would be the best looking guy, but God warned Samuel that He does not look at the outward appearance. Instead, God looks at the heart (See I Samuel 16:7). Oftentimes, we err in our assessment of people because we do not see the turmoil in their lives. We are not aware of the spiritual and emotional dilemmas they are dealing with. Never allow yourself to wallow in self-pity thinking that everyone else is getting ahead of you, and their life is better than yours based on what you see with your physical eyes. Material possessions should not define you.

There are some things we cannot prevent regardless of how hard we try. Relationships will grow cold, people we trust will forsake us and things we cherish will eventually go away. Nevertheless, we should hold on tightly to the eternal truth that God remains the same. He never changes. If you base your joy and peace on what you have and who is in your life, you will be disappointed. To do that will make your foundation shaky. Although these things are precious, they are only temporary. Furthermore, they cannot reach deep into your soul to heal the wounds of your heart. Only God can fill the emptiness in one's life. I assure you that it doesn't matter how much you have or accumulate in life, it will never be enough to fill or satisfy the void in the human heart. Quite frankly, only God can fill that kind of emptiness.

In my life, I've learned to thrive with much and with little (See Philippians 4:12). I don't wait until things are right to shout. I shout every day. I wake up declaring, "This is the day that the Lord has made. I will rejoice and be glad in it!" (See Psalm 118:24).

Bad Things and Good People

Life is not always fair. From time to time we find ourselves asking, "Why do bad things happen to good people?" Your thinking is that bad things should happen to people who do wrong, but that is just not always the case. You can do right all day long and bad things may still happen to you. It is also good to note that not all problems in life are related to sin. You can be a good and righteous person, yet experience trouble. As a matter of fact, in life, you and I don't really have to do anything bad to experience problems. This is something that is common to every man. It's called life.

In the Bible, we read the story of the young man who had been born blind and was healed by Jesus. The Pharisees did not see the amazing miracle because they were fixed on blaming someone. They speculated, "Who sinned, his father or his mother?" However, Jesus replied that no one had sinned, but this occurrence gave God a place to do a miracle for His glory (See John 9:2).

It would be wonderful for me to tell you that there comes a time when we will have no trouble in this life…that will only happen when life on earth ends. What I can tell you though is that as Christians, we have help in Christ when trouble and affliction comes our way. Jesus said in John 16:33, *"These things I have spoken unto you, that in me ye might have peace. In the world ye shall have tribulation: but be of good cheer; I have overcome the world."* Today, you may be in a situation where you wonder why bad things happened to you. You may ask why, in spite of all the precautions you took, you have a child with a life-threatening disease or a learning disability.

You may look at how other people have experienced positive results in their life, like the person who drinks alcohol and smokes, but their baby came out perfectly healthy! We do not have all the answers for why things happen in life, and we may come up with all types of theories on why God allows certain things to happen to good people. One thing we are sure of is that God works everything out for the good of those who trust Him and *"who are the called according to His purpose"* (Romans 8:28).

We need to repent of our small view of God, and ask Him to enlarge our vision. God wants us to exercise our faith and know that He is entirely trustworthy and desires the very best for us. Even though times will get tough He will give us the strength to live through every season, the good and bad. In all things, He's teaching us how to still praise Him no matter what.

Although we have a very good God, we are contending with an adversary, who never plays fair and preys on our weaknesses by seeking whom he may devour. *"Be sober, be vigilant; because your adversary the devil, as a roaring lion, walketh about, seeking whom he may devour"* (I Peter 5:8).

Don't think because you're doing the right thing in the right place, at the right time that the enemy is going to leave you alone. He's going to do what he does best: kill, steal, and destroy (See John 10:10). He wants to destroy those who have accepted Jesus as their Lord and Savior so that he can keep them burdened with the problems of this world and stop their testimony. Never forget that *"No weapon that is formed against thee shall prosper, and every tongue that shall rise against thee in judgment thou shall condemn..."* (Isaiah 54:17).

Furthermore, the adversary is not your friend. He appears as an angel of light to deceive you, attack your character, and spread lies about you. It is his nature to deceive, and he can only act accordingly. This is exactly what he did with Job. He went to God and accused Job of only serving Him because of all the wealth he had acquired. Not so. It is important we understand that troubles and trials do come to those who are godly, but we can be assured that our faith in God will see us through any situation.

The enemy will use every strategy to turn you against God to stop His plans for your life. That's why the Bible tells us to submit to God, resist the devil and he will flee (See James 4:8). Don't play games with satan. He is the enemy of

God, and his aim is to destroy you by any means necessary. You need to let him know that he does not have the final say so on your life.

The devil tried to defy the prophet of God, Elijah, at Mount Carmel. Elijah tested the prophets of Baal by challenging them to put a bullock on the altar of Baal and call for fire. The false prophets called upon the name of their god from morning to sundown but nothing happened (See I Kings 18:25-29).

Elijah then made an altar for the Lord from twelve stones representing the twelve tribes of Israel and laid the bullock over some wood on the altar. He dug a trench around the altar and ordered four barrels of water to be poured over the sacrifice several times. Then, at the time of the evening sacrifice, he called upon the name of the Lord.

> *And it came to pass at the time of the offering of the evening sacrifice, that Elijah the prophet came near, and said, Lord God of Abraham, Isaac, and of Israel, let it be known this day that thou art God in Israel, and that I am thy servant, and that I have done all these things at thy word. Hear me, O Lord, hear me, that this people may know that thou art the Lord God, and that thou hast turned their heart back again. Then the fire of the Lord fell, and consumed the burnt sacrifice, and the wood, and the stones, and the dust, and licked up the water that was in the trench. And*

when all the people saw it, they fell on their faces: and they said, The Lord, he is the God; the Lord, he is the God (I King 18:36-39).

Fire fell from heaven and consumed the sacrifice! God performed this astounding miracle to show who is Lord. We see in this story that the prophets of Baal had the audacity to stand against the living God. They felt that Baal had the power to show himself mightier than God Almighty. They did everything they could to get an answer. They danced for Baal, cried louder, cut themselves until blood poured out, but to no avail. It was all an exercise in futility because their god could not see nor hear their cry.

All the God of Elijah required of him was faith. His hands are not short that He cannot save, and His ears are not stopped that He cannot hear (See Isaiah 59:1). Elijah's prayer was heard and God answered. God revealed Himself to everyone present in a powerful manner.

Elijah was not a supernatural being; he was human just as we are. He trusted God to intervene in the situation at hand. God will do the same for you. He will show your enemies that He is on your side working on your behalf. The devil will throw everything at you, but God will not leave you.

Even though your faith may be as small as a mustard seed, please know that what the devil has meant for evil, God will use for your good. When the prophets of Baal have had their say, it's about to be God's turn! Like Elijah, Job was able to stand in confidence. He boldly declared, *"I know my redeemer liveth..."* (Job 19:25). He was determined to wait until his change came.

It's Not Over Until God Says So

At this point of your life's story, you may feel like you are losing, but the story is not over. God will write the last chapter of your life. Your latter years shall be better than your former years (See Haggai 2:9). Yes, better days are yet ahead.

So far, you may have made some missteps. Perhaps, you have encountered great trials and afflictions. People you love may have hurt you. You may have made some bad decisions that have affected your relationships with your family and others.

God believes in making something from the remnant of broken lives. He specializes in taking broken pieces and putting them back together and when God heals, He leaves no scars! We can truly be assured that God will strengthen and keep us through any situation we face. You may feel like you are being sifted right now, but it's not over.

The end of your story will be determined by your response to God. You decide whether you will have a happy ending by committing your life to Him. God is not waiting for you to be perfect to come to Him. Don't keep beating up yourself about your past mistakes because they are lessons for your future. God is going to bring His promises to pass in your life. Before you reap, you're going to sow by continuing to praise Him and to stand in faith (See Galatians 6:7).

The Lord Restores

Even when his wife told him to curse God and die, Job stood his ground (See Job 2:9). His response was "...*Thou speakest as one of the foolish women speaketh. What? shall we receive good at the hand of God, and shall we not receive evil? In all this did not Job sin with his lips*" (Job 2:10).

Although he did not curse God, he questioned the goodness of God in sending him evil. He could not figure out why God would allow such great affliction after living uprightly and ensuring his children were sanctified. For days and nights, Job was filled with pain and grief of not knowing why.

In our finite minds, we may think this entire situation was unfair to Job because we cannot see what God sees. There is nothing that happens to a child of God that goes unnoticed by Him. Jesus said that even the hairs on our heads are numbered (See Matthew 10:30). If a sparrow falls to the ground, God knows (See Matthew 10:29).

We are more precious to God than the sparrows. If He pays such meticulous attention to what happens to birds, how much more He cares for us!

God knew every detail of Job's life and how it would unfold. He had firsthand knowledge of the beginning and the end. He did not reveal the details to Job but only desired that Job remained faithful.

The time came in Job's life when God decided that he had faced enough afflictions. The same God who allowed the devil to bring about evil on Job was about to restore him. God is amazing, isn't He? Although He seemed far away, He was with Job throughout his entire ordeal. Ultimately, He is in control. If you remain faithful like Job, you will receive greater blessings. Let the former things go and trust God to multiply your blessings. If you stand still and wait on Him, He will give you double for your trouble.

Would Job have been restored if he had given up? Would he have been blessed with greater blessings if he had lost faith in God? Psalm 126:1-2 tells of the wonder and amazement of the Jewish captives when they were allowed to return to Jerusalem: *"When the Lord turned again the captivity of Zion, we were like them that dream"* (Psalm 126:1). They had to shake themselves awake to the reality that they were back in Jerusalem as free people. The air was filled with laughter and shouts of joy. Even the heathens proclaimed among the nations, *"...The Lord hath done great things for them"* (Psalm 126:2).

I encourage you to believe that the Lord will also do great things for you. Like the children of Zion, you have sown in tears, but the day will come when you will reap with joy, bearing praises to God (See Psalm 126:5-6). You may have watered your dreams with tears, but the day of reaping will come. You will remember the Lord's assurance that He will restore all the years the locust has eaten. He will restore your finances, family, joy, peace and the things you lost as a result of being sifted.

> *And I will restore to you the years that the locust hath eaten, the cankerworm, and the caterpiller, and the palmerworm, my great army which I sent among you* (Joel 2:25).

I don't like it when people around me complain when things are not going well for them. I like to have people who will smile and say in the midst of the challenge, "Preach the Word pastor, because the Word works." Honestly, I don't want you with me during my best times if I can't find you during my tough times.

One of the reasons Gwen married me was because of my great love for God. It was certainly not because of what I owned. At the time, we were very young and all I had was an old rugged car that chugged along. Now that I'm driving nicer cars and living in a bigger house, she's still the one who is by my side. I know she's the one I can count on. This is a common saying, "In prosperity, our friends know us; in adversity, we know our friends" (John Churton Collins). I am thankful I can say without a doubt that she is my best friend because she stands with me both in prosperity and in adversity.

Nevertheless, the greatest person to have throughout the changing seasons of life is God. He has never left me nor forsaken me. He was with me when I was down. He was with me when I was hurting. He was with me when I needed a job. Through it all, He has always been there.

You can be certain that the same way God who is always there for me, is there for you too. He will be in your life if you let Him. Just as He was with Job, Noah, Moses, Joseph, David, the disciples, and the early church, He is with you today. His plans and purpose for them were fulfilled as they yielded to Him.

You can see the plans for your life come to pass as you also submit to God. He will not leave you. *"Let your conversation be without covetousness; and be content with such things as ye have: for he hath said, I will never leave thee, nor forsake thee"* (Hebrews 13:5).

You Are a Comeback Kid

Sometimes we can be really hard on ourselves, focusing only on the negative things happening in our lives, that we fail see the good things happening as well. We become critical not only of our imperfections, but are also critical of other people and find fault with everything around us. It's time out to stop and see what God is doing. See the good things as well.

The Apostle Paul in his writing to the Romans told them: "The wages of sin is death, but the gift of God is eternal life through Christ Jesus our Lord" (Romans 6:23).

Here we see on one hand sin results in death, but on the other side of the story, Paul tells them they can have the free gift of eternal life through faith in Jesus Christ.

He goes on to say, *"But thanks be to God, which giveth us the victory through our Lord Jesus Christ."* (1 Corinthians 15:57).

Let us not forget Dr. Martin Luther King Jr back in the 1960's, in the face of prejudice and segregation, stood on the steps of a Montgomery courthouse fighting for voting rights and equality for African-Americans, declared: "How long? Not long."

"Like an idea whose time has come, not even the marching of mighty armies can halt us. We are moving to the land of freedom." (MLK)

Even though life was being viewed from the "valley," Dr. King saw into the future a view of life from the mountaintop, and declared "How long?" "Not long."

I was asking God, "Why do you want me to share about Job?" He impressed upon my heart to look up the meaning of the name "Job." I found that in Hebrew, Job's name means "come back." Job's destiny was already written in his name. God was letting him know that he was going to make a comeback.

The enemy has made you think you are going to be down forever. I'm letting you know right now that you are about to bounce back!

One day I was watching a Duke University basketball game with Coach Mike Krzyzewski as the head coach. Duke was down by 27 points, and the opposing team thought the game was going to be a win for them. They were already celebrating. Then, all of a sudden, it was time for the comeback. What didn't happen during the first through third quarters started to happen in the fourth quarter. Nothing was working, but suddenly everything turned around and Duke won the game! Maybe those first three quarters were your life's story up until last year. Nothing worked right, but it's about to turn around this year.

I was once miserable because of something I had to go through, but I had to realize that I'm a comeback kid. I kept on fighting. My weapon was to praise God. You need to give God praise for all that He has done and is doing in your life right now. He is the God of not only the second chance but the God of infinite chances. In fact, your Father owns the team you are on. You can swing as much as you need until you get a hit. Don't stop desiring to get it right.

Job also made this profound statement that you shall decree a thing, and it shall be established (See Job 22:28). What did he mean? When you make a decree, you are like the president making an executive order. When God's people act in His authority to decree or declare something, God will bring it to pass.

We have to decree some things and watch God move on our behalf. I remember making the decree, "my whole house shall be saved!" I also decreed that I will never be in want or broke another day of my life! I decreed that I was going to have more than enough to help somebody else and to sow into the Kingdom of God! I have decreed that I won't let my joy be stolen from me for I know that if the devil can't take my joy, he can't take my life.

Why not make a decree over your life right now?

Can you imagine Job saying this with his fist at the devil? "I know I'm Job. I am a comeback kid. I have a track record of coming in from the back, and I am already a winner!"

Can you also imagine a "comeback" woman whose husband has left her saying, "Oh, because you left me, you think I'm going to die? You think I am going to lose. With God's help, I am going to take better care of myself, and I will not let you cause me to lose hope. When you see me the next time, I will be looking just fine because I will not be defeated!"

Hear the words of Jesus:

And the Lord said, Simon, Simon, behold, Satan hath desired to have you, that he may sift you as wheat: But I have prayed for thee, that thy faith fail not: and when thou art converted, strengthen thy brethren (Luke 22:31-32).

The intention of satan was to shake Peter's faith and to disconnect Him from the vine so that he would be of no use to himself or to God. It is important to note that Jesus did not stop satan from attacking Peter, but His prayer was that Peter's faith would be strong enough to resist the enemy.

The fight you put up is more important than the attack. Jesus was confident that Peter would win because He said, *"when thou art converted"* not *"if."* After coming out of the sifting process victoriously, Peter's new role was to strengthen his brothers. Jesus repeated this command after His resurrection when He took Peter aside and told him, *"...Feed my lambs"* (John 21:15).

Don't be like Job's friends who judged him prematurely and tried to bring condemnation upon him. Be a true disciple of Jesus and show forth God's compassion towards those who are in pain. Remember, after you've made your comeback, help restore your friends and your brothers who are in dire straits. When you have come through this, you're going to be better than before.

God is real, and He is in control of all things relating to your life even when it doesn't seem like it in your eyes. When it doesn't make sense to you, you can still have confidence that your turnaround is coming. It won't always be like this; your best days are in front of you.

Like Job, you too can say, *"For I know that my redeemer liveth, and that he shall stand at the latter day upon the earth"* (Job 19:25). He will never leave nor forsake you (See Hebrews

13:3). The same God who is with you when things are going well is the same God who will stand by your side on the not so good days. He will come through for you as He did for Job.

Would you be surprised if I told you that you can make something out of nothing? *Nothing* means not anything, zero, of no value, not at all. So, how can you make something out of zero? With man it is impossible, but with God all things are possible.

In the beginning, nothing existed. God created *something* out of *nothing* when He made the world and all living things. Prior to that there was no universe, no time, space, matter nor light. Nothing, except God.

> *In the beginning God created the heavens and the earth. And the earth was formless and void, and darkness was over the surface of the deep; and the Spirit of God was moving over the surface of the waters. Then God said, "Let there be light"; and there was light* (Genesis 1:1-2).

Jesus continued this pattern when He walked the earth performing miracles.

> *On the third day, there was a marriage in Cana of Galilee and the mother of Jesus was there. And both Jesus was called and his disciples, to the marriage. And when they wanted wine, the mother Jesus saith to him, "They have no wine." Jesus saith to her, "Woman, what have I to do with thee? My hour is not yet come." His mother saith unto the servants, "Whatever he saith unto you, do it"* (John 2:1-5).

Here Jesus and his mother were invited to a wedding in Cana. This being a time of great celebration and joy, I can only imagine how devastating it was for the host to realize he ran out of wine for his guests. Of course, this could be quite embarrassing. When Jesus' mother learned of their predicament, she immediately addressed the matter with Jesus and asked for His help.

At first Jesus responded that this was not the time nor the place, but Mary knowing her Son and what He could do, took it on herself to instruct them to do "whatever Jesus tells them to do."

It is very likely that the servants at this wedding had no idea what Jesus was about to do when He told them to fill the jars with water (See John 2:7). They knew a problem existed and perhaps had their own thoughts about how it could be resolved. I can almost imagine the hesitant look on their faces and the possible doubt in their hearts when Jesus told them to fill the pots with water. Nevertheless, they did not object nor did they question Jesus' motives, but did what He instructed them to do.

Can you imagine if you were one of those servants, how you would have responded if Jesus, who at that time had never performed a public miracle, asked you to do something so strange? Would you have laughed at the request? Would you have doubted? Or, would you have spent time analyzing the situation and questioning Jesus' sanity?

Challenges in life are inevitable. A time will come in your life when you will face problems and situations that require power beyond your ability. How will you cope? What will you do?

These servants set a good example for us to follow, and we can learn a few lessons to help us navigate through our own tests and trials:

1. Don't try to logically analyze the problem.

2. Look to the Word for your solution.

3. Trust and obey whatever God tells you to do.

God does not lie. Unlike human beings, God can be trusted to keep His Word. You can be sure if He said He's going to do something in your life, He will do it. If He promised to supply your needs, He will draw from His infinite resources to deliver you. You must remember to uphold your end of the bargain by being obedient, always remembering that "to obey is better than sacrifice."

You can lose many opportunities in life if you fail to obey. The fulfillment of prophecies over your life can be delayed if you do not take the corresponding action God has revealed to you.

Walk in the Way God Commands

The story of the Israelites is filled with many examples of the results and consequences of obedience and disobedience to God. God made it clear to them that the

Promised Land was theirs, but because of their disobedience only Joshua and Caleb from that generation were able to enter the land. The others were barred because of their disobedience (See Hebrews 3:18).

If you are going to please God, obedience is key. We can only know God better and get closer to Him when we obey His Word, regardless of what your mind dictates. You can reap the rewards of obedience when you walk in faith.

When you make the choice to obey God, you can rest assured you are setting yourself up to experience His blessings. So often in life we desire to experience God's abundance but are not willing to submit to His will. On the contrary, to disobey God is to say you don't trust Him. Therefore, it's not enough to only know what He wants, but you must also do what He instructs, bearing in mind that *"Faith without works is dead"* (James 2:20).

It's Brim Time

As mentioned earlier, Jesus' mother told the servants to do whatever He says (See John 2:5). Jesus instructed them to fill the six water pots, *"...Fill the water pots with water..."* (John 2:7). And they filled them up to the brim. In other words, the pots were filled to capacity. They obeyed because they took Jesus at His Word and did just as He said.

I believe it is time for overflow in your life! Will you seize the opportunity and receive God's abundance? When you obey God, He will make it worth your while. Give it your all! Let the enemy know you're now walking in the overflow!

If you can believe and conceive it, then you can achieve it. God can do exceeding, abundantly, over and above all we can ask or imagine (See Ephesians 3:20).

As we face various challenges in our daily walk, we see in Joshua chapter 6 the story of God's people who, after suffering at the hands of the Egyptians and wandering in the wilderness some forty years because of their unbelief, now facing a Jericho experience. With no place to run or to hide, they had to look to God and followed His instructions to gain the victory. There was no turning back!

As a child of God, saved by the blood of Jesus, you must know your identity in Christ and daily affirm your faith:

> *I'm born again. I'm not trying to earn my salvation. I received it by faith through grace. I'm filled with the Holy Spirit who is leading me into all truth. I have the revelation that I am seated in heavenly places in Christ, far above all the works of darkness. I am more than a conqueror in Christ. This is who I'm going to be the rest of my life. I am no longer a baby Christian but growing stronger in faith according to the profession of my faith. I have dedicated my life to God, and I belong to God.*

No matter what you face, do not allow anything to turn you aside from this truth.

To do this is to keep your vessel filled to the brim. When Jesus turned the water into wine, He took what seemed like nothing and made it into the best wine they had ever tasted. It's time to start with what you have and allow God to multiply and use it for His glory.

Something in Your Nothing

If you feel you have nothing to offer such as a particular skill, talent or even money, be encouraged. In Genesis 1, we see a vivid description of how God created the heavens and the earth. The earth was without form and void, but He spoke words to bring light and life to the universe.

I once visited an art exhibition and was drawn to two paintings. They were worth thousands of dollars and had already been sold. As I gazed at these paintings, I mused on the thought of how their origin was nothing but a blank piece of canvas. However, it took the artistry of the painter to make something of no value become so valuable that art collectors would outbid each other to own a piece.

Likewise, your hand in God's hand will add value to your life when you place them where God tells you to. What are your skills? What do you do best? Painting? Cooking? Teaching? Well, guess what? Whatever your skills, God wants you to use it not just for His glory but to increase you.

Once you use what He has blessed you with, you'll begin to see increase. God said in Jeremiah 29:11, *"For I know the thoughts that I think toward you, saith the Lord, thoughts of peace, and not of evil, to give you an expected end."* God has great things in store for you.

In Jeremiah chapter 18, God sent the prophet Jeremiah to the potter's house to teach him a valuable lesson. He used the analogy of a potter at work on clay making and molding it into the vessel he wanted. During the process, it became marred, but the potter never discarded the clay. Rather, he took it again, reshaped and remolded it until it became the vessel he wanted it to be.

Before a potter starts working on clay, he has a good idea what he wants to form. He has already formulated in his mind what he expects the finished work to look like. Similarly, God, the great Potter, knows what He wants to make of you. He has great plans and an intended outcome for you.

As you remain in His hands, the process of making you into a vessel of honor will not always be smooth. Sometimes, like clay, you may resist the shape that God wants to make you. However, you will soon learn that God's purpose must prevail.

When you remain in His hands and allow the process to reach completion, you will be revealed as the unique and special creation you are. Hebrews 11:3 (NLT) says, *"By faith we understand that the entire universe was formed at God's command, that what we now see did not come from anything that can be seen."*

Having Faith in Nothingness

"Now, faith is the substance of things hoped for the evidence of things not seen" (Hebrews 11:1). From this verse we see that faith is a substance, not an abstract quality. In other words, it is faith that produces something from nothing. Faith is the substance or evidence we need for things to come into existence. Faith takes things hoped for and makes them a reality in the natural realm.

The substance of faith, the ability to see something that was not there, enabled the Old Testament elders to live in joyful expectation of what God had promised. Although most of those promises were not realized in their lifetime, they were totally convinced they would materialize by faith.

> *These all died in faith, not having received the promises, but having seen them afar off, and were persuaded of them, and embraced them, and confessed that they were strangers and pilgrims on the earth* (Hebrews 11:13).

The elders all obtained a good report because the things they saw and deposited in their spirits by faith were not made by the things that were tangible. In other words, nothing was made by things that could be seen or touched. Everything was made by things that were invisible.

The faith message continues in Isaiah 55:1 with this faith invitation, *"Ho, everyone that thirsts, come ye to the waters, and he that hath no money; come ye, buy, and eat; yea, come, buy wine and milk without money and without price."*

The prophet Isaiah made a great proclamation to everyone in need of spiritual blessing and sustenance. He invited them to have their needs met without paying a monetary price. It would not be a surprise if many people who heard Isaiah's invitation rejected it as a hoax.

Some may have laughed at him asking, "How in the world am I going to buy all those things without money? What system of exchange are they using?" Isaiah was offering something that was not easy to receive with the natural mind. Truly, it takes faith to believe that you can have something of such value and importance for free.

Always remember that nothing is too hard for God. He will fulfill whatever He has promised.

> *So shall my word be that goeth forth out of my mouth: it shall not return unto me void, but it shall accomplish that which I please, and it shall prosper in the thing whereto I sent it* (Isaiah 55:11).

Speak the Word of God

God's Word will never return to Him void. He will bring it to pass in your life when you speak His Word over your life. By faith, we call those invisible things as if they already existed.

> *But without faith it is impossible to please him: for he that cometh to God must believe that he is, and that he is a rewarder of them that diligently seek him* (Hebrews 11:6).

If we really want to please God, we must have faith. Jesus walked the earth, and He encountered people who did and did not believe. The people of Jesus' hometown robbed themselves of a great opportunity to experience the miraculous and mighty power of God in their families and community because of unbelief. Although Jesus had healed the sick, cleansed lepers, cast out demons, and opened the blind eyes of many people, He could not do many great works when He arrived at Nazareth (See Mark 6:5).

In Mark 9:20-23, the father of a boy possessed by an evil spirit came to Jesus for help. He had obviously heard of Jesus' great miracles:

> *And they brought him unto him: and when he saw him, straightway the spirit tare him; and he fell on the ground, and wallowed foaming. And he asked his father, How long is it ago since this came unto him? And he said, Of a child. And ofttimes it hath cast him into the fire, and into the waters, to destroy him: but if thou canst do anything, have compassion on us, and help us. Jesus said unto him, If thou canst believe, all things are possible to him that believeth.*

As the father approached Jesus and explained his predicament, he asked a question which exposed the condition of his faith. He said to Jesus, "Help my son, if you can." Note the words, "If you can." It seems that Jesus was somewhat taken aback by those words and He responded, "If you can believe." In other words, "What do you mean if I can?" "Of course, I can! The real question is "Do you believe?"

The same question is being asked of you today. "Do you believe?" It is not God's fault that you are not successful or that you are not making progress in the areas you would like. He is *not* the reason you are not attaining your goals and dreams. You must ask yourself if you truly believe what God has said about you. Think about it and answer honestly.

Let's look at Moses as an example. After fleeing Egypt and living at the backside of the desert for forty years, Moses felt there was not anything left for him to accomplish. Many years of his life had passed, and his hopes and dreams seemed to have faded. On the other hand, God did not see it the same way. He saw what He purposed for Moses. He saw destiny fulfilled. He saw a new beginning.

Moses was given the assignment to approach Pharaoh and demand the freedom of the Israelites. Initially, he was afraid, but by faith he was able to see the plan of God and rise above the fear. *"By faith he forsook Egypt, not fearing the wrath of the king: for he endured, as seeing him who is invisible"* (Hebrews 11:27).

Because it would seem like the human brain is geared to fear, it is our tendency when something happens to allow our minds to go to the worst case scenario. But it is time to renew our minds, rise above every fear, and soar in the things God has purposed for you.

See It in the Spirit First

There is a physical and a spiritual realm. Everything we see in this physical realm was first birthed in the spiritual realm. It begins with an idea, a dream, or a vision. You first have to see and receive it in your spirit before you have it in the natural. When the Spirit of God indwells the believer, he or she then has the ability to see from a spiritual perspective.

Jesus said to Nicodemus, *"I tell you the truth, no one can see the kingdom of God unless he is born again"* (John 3:3). Furthermore, the apostle Paul told the believers in the church at Ephesus:

> *I pray that the eyes of your heart may be enlightened in order that you may know the hope to which he has called you, the riches of his glorious inheritance in his holy people, and his incomparably great power for us who believe. That power is the same as the mighty strength* (Ephesians 1:18-19).

The Bible declares in 1 Cor. 2:9–15:

> *But as it is written: 'Eye has not seen, nor ear heard, nor have entered into the heart of man the things which God has prepared for those who love Him.' But God has revealed them to us through His Spirit.*

> *For the Spirit searches all things, yes, the deep things of God. For what man knows the things of a man except the spirit of the man which is in him? Even so no one knows the things of God except the Spirit of God. Now we have received, not the spirit of the world, but the Spirit who is from God, that we might know the things that have been freely given to us by God. These things we also speak, not in words which man's wisdom teaches but which the Holy Spirit teaches, comparing spiritual things with spiritual. But the natural man does not receive the things of the Spirit of God, for they are foolishness to him; nor can he know them, because they are spiritually discerned. But he who is spiritual judges all things, yet he himself is rightly judged by no one.*

It is important to open your eyes and see in the Word of God a realm that is invisible to the natural mind, and thereby learn to operate more in the realm of the Spirit. God told Joshua, "I have given all this land to you" (See Joshua 1:2-6). They were still on the other side of the Jordan outside of Canaan. It belonged to Joshua as soon as God spoke it out of His mouth. Unfortunately, the nation of Israel didn't recognize that victory was already in their hands.

Your enemy is defeated. Everything that God has promised you is in your hands. The enemy is in denial that he has already been defeated. There is no rematch because it's over. Victory belongs to us. The Bible says, "...*shout to God with the voice of triumph*" (Psalm 47:1).

You can have confidence that your enemy is a defeated foe. Victory belongs to Jesus, therefore you have the victory, walk in it!"

Every day we get up, we look in the mirror. Why? Because by doing this we get to see a physical reflection of who we are. Women look in the mirror to put on make-up and fix their hair. Men look in the mirror to shave and check attire. We do this because we all want to make sure our clothes fit, our hair is in place and we look right before we step out to face the world.

But what do you *really* see when you look in the mirror? No doubt you may see imperfections, flaws, failure, disappointments, weaknesses, fear. But that is not what God wants you to see. He wants you to see what He sees. He wants you to see the reflection of His beloved Son Jesus Christ shining through. Yes, He wants you to see future, potential, strength and hope.

Yes, you may be looking a little rough on the edges right now, but nonetheless there is a beautiful diamond beneath the surface.

Diamond? Yes! Diamonds are precious gems that can be very expensive. Also, there are diamonds and there are *rare* diamonds. But do you know how a diamond is made?

Recently, I did some research on the formation of diamonds and discovered that diamonds are formed deep below the earth's crust. Diamonds are created as a result of intense heat and pressure. It starts out as a piece of coal and is composed of carbon as well as graphite. Carbon is hard, but graphite is soft. While the diamond is the hardest mineral known to man, graphite is one of the softest of substances. The diamond is transparent, but graphite is opaque. Additionally, a diamond is known to be an excellent electrical insulator, while graphite is a good conductor of electricity.

How can two materials of the same chemical composition be so different? While the diamond is so rare, its basic constituent, carbon, can be found everywhere.

One is quite valuable and can be found at jewelry stores, and the other is simply commonplace. But even though the coal is seen as common, there is something beautiful on the inside that only comes out after it has been processed a certain way.

Like coal, we sometimes see ourselves as common and ordinary. But I want you to know that there is absolutely no reason for you to feel like you are less than, ordinary or common, because in God's eyes you are precious and of great value. So much so that Jesus paid a great price for you.

A price He paid with His life, because you are one-of-a-kind! Because you are worth the precious blood of Jesus! Because you are worth dying for.

> *Are not five sparrows sold for two copper coins? And not one of them is forgotten before God. But the very hairs of your head are all numbered. Do not fear therefore; you are of more value than many sparrows* (Luke 12:6-7).

You are His precious jewel! *"They shall be Mine,'* says the Lord of hosts, *"On the day that I make them my jewel"* (Malachi 3:17).

If you are to become the gem of a diamond kind of person God made you to be, it will not always be easy. It is a process. A shaping and a making from what was to what can be.

Sometimes you don't know how much work needs to be done in your life until you are fully in God's hands. It is only in the light of His presence that you are able to see how inadequate you really are without Him.

Just like a diamond starts out as a piece of coal, seeming to be of little value until it goes through the pressure process, likewise to the world, and sometimes in your very own eyes, you are seen as ordinary and not worth much. But God sees so much more.

I want you to know that with the Lord Jesus on your side indwelling your life, there is no telling what you can do or become - the possibilities are truly limitless! But to get to that place called 'there' you need a new mindset.

> *Do not conform to the pattern of this world, but be transformed by the renewing of your mind. Then you will be able to test and approve what God's will is—his good, pleasing and perfect will* (Romans 12:2).

I loved Michael Jackson and the words of a favorite song of his goes like this:

> *I'm starting with the man in the mirror,*
> *I'm asking him to change his ways*
> *And no message could have been any clearer*
> *If you want to make the world a better place*
> *Take a look at yourself, and then make a change.*

He went on to say, *"I'm gonna make a change, gonna make a difference, make it right."*

Yes, it really does start with the man in the mirror, *you*. Yes, take a step into your future. Make a change. Make a difference. *"I can do all things through Christ who strengthens me."* (Philippians 4:13).

Humility Is Admirable

Humility is a characteristic that God admires. It's important to remain humble when you have achieved your dreams and things are going well. But never for a moment think you did it on your own. Always remember to take heed when you are standing so you don't fall.

> *Therefore, let anyone who thinks he stands [who feels sure that he has a steadfast mind and is standing firm], take heed lest he fall [into sin] (1 Corinthians 10:12).*

Just like a diamond, you and I come from humble beginnings, from the dust of the earth and we were completely lifeless until God through His mighty power breathed life into our bodies and we became living beings. Without God, we are nothing.

The psalmist David had a special trait called humility. Throughout the Bible, it is easy to see that he was quick to acknowledge his sins and prayed for forgiveness. He asked God to search his heart, look deep within and expose wicked thoughts. He went a step further and asked God to cleanse and purge him.

> *There hath no temptation taken you but such as is common to man: but God is faithful, who will not suffer you to be tempted above that ye are able; but will with the temptation also make a way to escape, that ye may be able to bear it* (I Corinthians 10:13).

You Are Not Going Under

We all experience difficulties and struggles in life. Sometimes when faced with these situations, you may feel like no one is there for you or even that no one is listening, but believe me, Jesus Christ knows everything you're going through, and He alone can truly help give you the peace of mind you need to endure.

Whatever it is, it may be that you are at a place in your life when you think you are about to drown. Your finances, health and relationships may be broken, and all bent out of shape but you are not going under. God will make a way of escape. You will become stronger and wiser, and He will empower you to handle every circumstance. You can go through your trials and rise above each and every one of them.

When God says, "not now," He does not mean "not ever." He is simply saying that for the moment or season, you will need to patiently wait on Him. His timing is never wrong. Some successes take longer than others. Some battles are harder to win than others, but it does not mean you will not succeed or conquer. God may just be saying, "Wait."

> *But they that wait upon the Lord shall renew their strength; they shall mount up with wings as eagles; they shall run, and not be weary; and they shall walk, and not faint* (Isaiah 40:31).

During the hard times in life, don't let the enemy steal your joy. Don't become depressed and dismayed about your situation because the Lord is on your side. I want you to know that you can make it through the rough waters knowing that God is grooming you for something better.

Life can be a bumpy ride, and reshaping and remodeling are necessary for the process. At certain intervals, the Potter has to put us back on the wheel of life for correction. Sometimes it means going back to the place where we started. If so, your return to the past is only for you to be motivated to move forward. Not to dwell there. Take the good things you can from it and press forward to a brighter path.

You Are Set Apart

Many of us lose our identity very early in life, and the uniqueness of our personalities fade because we are expected to be a certain way. Regardless, you are a diamond! God made each of us with different talents and abilities. We all have unique personalities and characteristics that make us who we are. And certainly, each of us is marvelously and wonderfully created by God: *"I will praise thee; for I am fearfully and wonderfully made: marvellous are thy works; and that my soul knoweth right well"* (Psalm 139:14).

It is easy to look at this verse from the viewpoint of your physical features. However, beauty goes beyond our outward appearance because true beauty comes from deep within our inner being. No matter how beautiful we may be on the outside, we all have flaws and insecurities that we hide from others. But in spite of these shortcomings, we are still remarkable beings because God made us in His image and likeness.

He created us to resemble Him. Of all God's creations He chose us to look like Him and have communion and dominion with Him. Isn't that wonderful? Can you appreciate your uniqueness, and how special you are to God? Again, your resemblance to God has nothing to do with your physical appearance but everything to do with your spiritual self. You were made in God's image, meaning you can think, reason, and be righteous and holy.

God has set you apart from other creatures, and you are distinctly different from other humans. Your uniqueness should not be hidden but used to glorify God. You are a masterpiece. As we combine our special gifts, characteristics, and abilities, we can work together to advance the Kingdom of God. Each morning you should look at yourself in the mirror saying, "I am brilliant. God's radiance is shining through me today."

Four C's of Diamonds

Have you ever looked at yourself from the perspective of a diamond? All diamonds have four C's or properties. These 4 C's represent the four main components of a diamond's beauty and structure: Clarity, Color, Carat and Cut. These are the four components which is used to determine the price of how valuable each piece of diamond is worth.

Clarity. A diamond is real because you can see through it, and light passes through which causes it to sparkle.

Can others see the Light in your life? The Bible says that Jesus is *"the light of the world"* (John 8:12), and we *"shine as lights in the world"* (Philippians 2:15).

Clarity also means profound insight. God will give you divine insight to pray for people and situations. *"But strong meat belongs to them that are of full age, even those who by reason of use have their senses exercised to discern both good and evil"* (Hebrews 5:14).

Color. Gem-quality diamonds occur in many colors, ranging from colorless to light yellow or light brown. Colorless diamonds are the rarest.

Color represents your true self; the self that has regained authenticity and uniqueness just as every diamond is unique. This is the deep realization that you are one of a kind, never to be duplicated. You should not live someone else's life. The Word of God warns us about the folly of comparing ourselves with others:

> *We do not dare to classify or compare ourselves with some who commend themselves. When they measure themselves by themselves and compare themselves with themselves, they are not wise*
> (II Corinthians 10:12, NIV).

If you choose to compare yourself to others, then you do not recognize or appreciate your uniqueness. The combination of your physical, mental, and spiritual characteristics belongs to you. *"You are fearfully and wonderfully made"* (Psalm 139:14).

Carat. The third C of a diamond is carat which represents weight. Its value is based on the size.

Cut. The kind of cut will make all the difference between an exquisitely fashioned diamond whose multi-facets reflect the light, and a rough dull-looking stone of little value.

Who have you allowed to cut you? Have you allowed people and painful episodes in your life to cut into your soul? Have you been cut by guilt and shame? Have you allowed things or people to make you rough and dull?

Your character reveals who you are. It's not how you look on the outside but who you are on the inside that really matters. The Bible says that man judges by outward appearances, but God deals with the heart.

Did you know that the only tool that can cut a diamond is another diamond? You may feel comfortable in the company of the cubic zirconia, but they can't cut, mold, inspire or challenge you, because they are fake diamonds without the cutting edge. Apart from the cubic zirconia looking like a diamond, they have very little in common

As an individual, it is vital to be in the company of those who have similar core values. Diamonds need to hang with diamonds to be cut into the image of who you are destined to be. Right now, you may simply be a diamond in the rough, but your moment to sparkle and shine is ahead of you on the other side of now.

It is important that you speak life into every situation by declaring the promises of God for your life. As you continue to declare His Word, the truth will be cemented in your spirit and bring renewal to your mind. Once your mind is renewed with the Word of God, your actions will line up and follow. As you consistently affirm God's Word, you will begin to see manifestation.

If you are under pressure right now, then don't continue to use the methods that have failed you in the past. The acclaimed genius Albert Einstein said, "The definition of insanity is doing the same thing over and over again and expecting a different result." This is also applicable to how you handle your problems when under pressure. Don't go back to the place of defeat. Avoid calling yourself a failure and withdrawing from friends and loved ones. Try something different, by going against what you feel inclined to do naturally.

As a pastor, I have been asked numerous times, "How do you preach like you do?" My answer is always very simple: "I have experienced tremendous pressure." Yes, I have been in situations I could not handle by myself and had to rely totally on God all the way through it all. Therefore, regardless of what it looks like, I have learned that with God on my side, I am an overcomer.

Rejoice! You may not look like it right now, but you are a diamond. You value is way more than a dollar amount. Sure, you may not be where you need to be, but neither are you where you used to be. You are a unique masterpiece carved in the likeness of Christ and you're about to shine like never before!

It's Time to Shine

God's children are called to shine – to reflect a brightness that is beyond ourselves. "Let your light so shine *before men, that they may see your good works, and glorify your Father which is in heaven"* (Matthew 5:16). The Bible tells us there is a time for everything. Yes, you may have walked in darkness before, but that was then, and this is now! The life you now live is one of destiny and purpose, and the purpose of light is to shine.

I don't know about you, but I'm at that point in my life where I am shining. The very Light of Christ shines through me, influencing and drawing others to Jesus, not only in church or in my family or circle of friends, but everywhere I go I am fulfilling the commission to let my light shine even in the midnight hour when things are looking bleak and hopeless.

Are you perfect? No. But just like the diamond, if you look closely you will see imperfections, but only the Lord Himself can expertly cut away all your imperfections to reveal the beautiful hidden facets on the inside you did not even know were there. Not only are you an expertly cut diamond, you are priceless and of the highest value, ready to shine in any situation.

Don't be alarmed at this point in your life if you are not exactly where you had hoped to be. Know that not only has God carved you out, but He has to also cut some people out of your life, so that you can be transparent and shine.

Some of those being removed are the people you thought you needed the most for your comfort and security. Now you are no longer dependent on them, so you can shine as never before and do the things you never thought possible.

The loss of some of the crutches you have depended upon may initially be painful, but with time you will understand why God made the shifts to rearrange your life. The Bible teaches that God will not prevent you from having anything that is good (See Psalm 84:11). So, don't be anxious or get confused. Just know that God is working everything out in your best interest.

Having the Right Motives

The color of a diamond has value which represents character. Our motives for doing things are vital and they matter. In all you do, ask God to give you pure motives. A pure motive is not the spectacular thing you do in the public arena. It's the small thing you do in your private world that no one sees.

Have you ever dealt with people who have the wrong motives? Do you know what they are like? They are cubic zirconia. They have hidden agendas and live according to the motto, "Fake it until you make it." You do not need to fake who you are in Him. Faith is not about being false and dishonest. It is about calling those things which do not exist in this realm as though they already are manifested.

If you are not your true self, then you are pretending. If you have never been under any pressure, you can't really understand the process of refinement. You will try to look impressive, but you will really only be an imitation.

Genuine people add beauty and value to life. They make the world better through acts of benevolence done from the heart. With sincerity they love, give, care, and spread joy.

God has called us to be the light of the world, not for our fame or popularity. He does not want us to help others so we can be placed on a pedestal. Actually, Jesus gave clear instructions on how we should be charitable:

> *Take heed that ye do not your alms before men, to be seen of them: otherwise ye have no reward of your Father which is in heaven. Therefore when thou doest thine alms, do not sound a trumpet before thee, as the hypocrites do in the synagogues and in the streets, that they may have glory of men. Verily I say unto you, They have their reward. But when thou doest alms, let not thy left hand know what thy right hand doeth: That thine alms may be in secret: and thy Father which seeth in secret himself shall reward thee openly* (Matthew 6:1-4).

Ultimately, our good deeds should be for the benefit of humanity and the glory of God. When we act with sincerity, God promises to reward us.

God Is Making You Better

There was a particular diamond mined in Africa which was the largest ever found. An ordinary person could not cut it; they had to find a master cutter. The cutter took a year to study, look at its features and put it under great scrutiny to get the perfect cut. It took patience to produce the quality they desired.

Likewise, God is patiently working on you. You may have prayed about your life and your circumstances repeatedly, but it seems nothing has changed. You are unable to determine why God hasn't done anything about it yet. He said, "I need to set you apart because I have to cut you just right."

Bear Bryant, the celebrated coach of Alabama Crimson Tide, was a real no-nonsense fellow. His team was playing against the University of South Carolina (USC) and was ahead by six points with only forty seconds left in the game. Bryant called in the quarterback, "I want you to just grab the ball and lay down." The quarterback decided on a different strategy; he was going to surprise them. He grabbed the ball and threw a pass. The opposing team's cornerback was quick to intercept it and was running to the end for a touchdown when suddenly Bryant's quarterback ran him down and tackled him on the five-yard line.

Bryant's quarterback saved the game. The opposing coach said, "Mr. Bryant, that quarterback, he ain't that fast.

How come he caught my man?" Bryant replied, "Your man was only running for six points. My man was running for his life because he knew I was going to kick his behind!"

Are you going to church and running just for the sake of it? Or, are you running to church to save your life? If you are desperate to serve God, have an intimate relationship with Him, hunger and thirst after His righteousness and long to be in His presence, you will not be disappointed. God promises to fill you and meet your physical and spiritual needs. He promised the woman at the well satisfaction for her discontented soul that only He could give (See John 4:14). Likewise, He promises you the same.

Thank God right now that He is molding you. Thank Him that even though you've been through some tough experiences. He is polishing the diamond and making you glitter and shine.

The potter in Jeremiah Chapter 18 took the clay and then put it aside because it was marred. That means it was worn. Are you worn out? Have you been broken? God sees that you are worn out and heartbroken. He knows the issues you face every day and wants to put you back on the wheel. Don't feel bad about yourself because He needs to refashion you into something better. The fact that He would take the time to reshape you shows the love He has for you and His commitment to make your life beautiful and complete.

I encourage you when you are weary to know that God is patiently working on you. Will you thank God for cutting you to make you a diamond of great price? Will you live in thanksgiving and recognize your value and worth? Speak to yourself, "I am one of a kind. No one else can be me. You're looking at an original gem exposed to intense heat and pressure. I have been carefully studied, cut and polished in the hands of the Master Cutter!"

Just like you are a unique and one-of-a-kind person, so is your story. It is not yet complete and each and every day as it develops, know that it is worth telling what God has done for you and how God has brought you out, to bring you into the other side of *your story*...for His glory!

About the Author

Bishop Donald E. Battle, one of today's most influential Christian leaders, is a dynamic and anointed man of God, full of faith, boldness and integrity. His practical style of preaching is marked by a unique blend of inspiration, challenge and humor that has touched the lives of many.

Bishop Battle has served as a member of the United States Army (MP) as well as a former City of Atlanta Police Detective and, for the last 28 years, Senior Pastor of Divine Faith Ministries International (DFMI). Under his leadership, God has abundantly blessed the ministry and DFMI has experienced unprecedented membership growth from 60 people in 1990 to a current membership of over 8,000, with campuses in Jonesboro, Barnesville, McDonough and Suwanee, Georgia.

He is also the Founder and President of International Covenant Christian Churches (i3C) Ministerial Fellowship. Through Joseph's Warehouse Outreach ministry, DFMI has become the number one distributor of food and clothing in Clayton County and surrounding communities.

A native of Fairfield, Alabama, Bishop Battle met and married his high school sweetheart and wife of 45 years, Gwen Battle, Pastor of DFMI's Suwanee campus. To their union, they have been blessed with three beautiful daughters: Pastor TaVondria Battle, Jamie Howard and Christin Smith, all of whom work within the ministry in some capacity, and seven precious grandchildren.

A visionary leader with a genuine love for people, Bishop Battle continues to minister throughout the U.S. and abroad. His message of faith and belief that with God ALL things are possible is what gives him the fervor and fortitude to preach the Gospel with boldness! This awesome man of God continues to speak life to the lost and hope to the broken-hearted and will not stop until he has impacted the world for Jesus Christ!

To contact Bishop Battle regarding speaking engagements, please use the information below.

Bishop Donald E. Battle
Divine Faith Ministries International
9800 Tara Blvd.
Jonesboro, GA 30236
770-603-0025
www.divinefaith.org

www.ingramcontent.com/pod-product-compliance
Lightning Source LLC
Chambersburg PA
CBHW030330080526
44584CB00012B/796